WORDSWORTH

William Wordsworth was born in Cockermouth, on the coast of the Lake District, in 1770, the second of five children. His rural upbringing inspired much of his poetry, and some of his most intense emotional passages, notably in *The Prelude*, stem from childhood and adolescent experience. As a young man, Wordsworth was fired with enthusiasm for the French Revolution. After graduating from Cambridge in 1791 he spent a year in France, where he had an affair with Annette Vallon. The later course of the Revolution left him disillusioned with radical politics, and on his return to England he devoted himself to literature, helped by the inheritance of a legacy. He met Coleridge in 1795 and the two men became intimate friends, though they were estranged between 1810 and 1812 on account of a drawn-out quarrel.

In 1799 Wordsworth settled in the Lake District with his sister Dorothy, who was a close companion for most of his life and shared his deep love of nature. He married Mary Hutchinson in 1802 and they had five children. Although his early work was not well received, his reputation grew steadily throughout his career. In 1813 he was appointed Distributor of Stamps for Westmorland, which enabled him to continue writing on a regular income. He became Poet Laureate seven years before his death in 1850.

The poetry that Wordsworth wrote before 1807 is now universally recognized as his finest work, but it was widely criticized at the time of publication. His simple and direct style, adopted in the belief that poetry should reflect the ordinary emotions of ordinary people, met with scorn, though his sonnets and odes show that he was also a master of the Grand Manner. Few of his first readers shared his conviction that the spiritual and natural worlds are interrelated, but the poems which express this theme have since been acclaimed as some of the finest pieces of verse in the English language.

December 25, 1988

Wordsworth

Poems

Selected by W.E. Williams

Introduction by Jenni Calder

PENGUIN BOOKS

Penguin Books Ltd, 27 Wrights Lane, London W8 5TZ (Publishing and Editorial)
and Harmondsworth, Middlesex, England (Distribution and Warehouse)
Viking Penguin Inc., 40 West 23rd Street, New York, New York 10010, USA
Penguin Books Australia Ltd, Ringwood, Victoria, Australia
Penguin Books Canada Ltd, 2801 John Street, Markham, Ontario, Canada L3R 1B4
Penguin Books (NZ) Ltd, 182–190 Wairau Road, Auckland 10, New Zealand

This selection first published 1943
Revised edition 1950
Reprinted 1954
Reissued with a new introduction 1985
Reprinted 1986, 1987

Printed and bound in Great Britain by
Cox & Wyman Ltd, Reading
Typeset in Monotype Caslon
Introduction reset at the University Press, Cambridge

Contents

CONTENTS

INTRODUCTION

BORN in Cumberland in 1770, Wordsworth went to Hawkshead Grammar School, where he was allowed considerable freedom to roam the countryside and come close to the life of country people. He went to Cambridge in 1787, and was in France in 1790, the year after the fall of the Bastille. He was profoundly influenced by the French Revolution, and returned to France, where his affair with Annette Vallon produced a child but no marriage. Wordsworth was later tormented by guilt and confusion, increased by the ensuing war between France and England, which shook his political convictions. These feelings are at the root of much of his poetry. With his sister Dorothy, who was very close to him, Wordsworth settled in Dorset. At this time he began his long and intimate association with Coleridge, and in 1798 they published *Lyrical Ballads*, which included Coleridge's 'Ancient Mariner' and Wordsworth's 'Tintern Abbey', a meditative poem in which he relates his response to nature to his past and present sensibilities, as well as a number of lyrics and verse anecdotes. This volume announced a radically new approach to the writing of poetry, which, although Wordsworth is often considered to be the father of the Romantic movement, bears little relation to what is conventionally termed Romantic. In the preface to the second edition (1800) Wordsworth stated his belief that neither the language nor the content of poetry should be stylized or elaborate and that the value of the poet was his ability to feel and express the relation between man and nature. In his own poetry this was worked out in the calm remembrance of tumultuous experiences, which resulted in drawing from this discrepancy a resolution that yielded universal perceptions of humanity and the natural world.

In 1799 Wordsworth and Dorothy returned to the Lake District to live in Dove Cottage, Grassmere. Coleridge also settled in the district. Three years later Wordsworth married

Mary Hutchinson. A long drawn-out quarrel with Coleridge and a decline in Dorothy's health disturbed the security that came with middle age. His reputation had grown, and in 1813 he was appointed Stamp Distributor, a sinecure that guaranteed him an income while he wrote. He became Poet Laureate in 1843.

At his best he wrote with a power that came from his fresh clarity of diction, and from a moving directness in his grappling with experience. Some of his early ballads are marred by the inappropriate use of an essentially simple and narrative form which could not easily accommodate the compound of description and moral message that Wordsworth was presenting. But at times his simple statements of elemental emotions, as in 'The Idiot Boy', were startling in their effect. But he was more successful in poems such as 'Michael' (1800) or 'The Old Cumberland Beggar' (1800), both poems rooted in his sympathetic experience of the intrinsic strength of country people, where the more solemn rhythm and the language that is direct and unadorned without the bareness of some earlier poems lends a more measured and thoughtful tone to the writing. The result is both more intense and more suggestive. His sonnets and lyrical recollections in tranquillity are probably his best-known poems – 'Composed upon Westminster Bridge', 'The Solitary Reaper', 'I Wandered Lonely as a Cloud', all published in the *Poems in Two Volumes* of 1807. They illuminate moments of particular perception with a general sense of universal meaning, while his famous ode, 'Intimations of Immortality from Recollections of Early Childhood' (1807), presents both an explanation and a representation of the balance of experience and reflection. This is a fuller and more directed treatment of the 'Tintern Abbey' theme. Wordsworth traces his developing personality and understanding from earliest childhood and draws from the relations to the natural world fundamental human truths, 'thoughts that do often lie too deep for tears'.

Wordsworth's long autobiographical poem, *The Prelude* (ed. J. C. Maxwell, Penguin Books), often considered his masterpiece, was not published until after his death. He had begun it in 1798 and had revised it continually throughout his life. It had been intended as an introduction to a long philosophical poem called 'The Recluse', of which only one part, 'The Excursion', was completed. In *The Prelude* there are passages of sustained intensity and excitement, particularly in Book 1, describing his childhood, which show Wordsworth at his best. Although much of the linking narrative is not on such an inspired level, the rhythmic energy and the variety of incidents and states of mind hold the reader's interest.

Wordsworth's critical writings are important documents in the history of critical thought. His preface to the second edition of *Lyrical Ballads* (1800) contains his famous account of the nature of poetry which he derives from his view of the psychology of the poet and the process of poetic composition. The poet is 'a man speaking to men', but a man 'endowed with more lively sensibility, more enthusiasm and tenderness, who has a greater knowledge of human nature, and a more comprehensive soul' than ordinary people. The poet also is particularly 'affected... by absent things as if they were present'. Wordsworth's view that the mind of man had, because of its very structure, a deep relationship with the forces at work in the world of external nature, and that those forces in the last analysis represented 'joy', gave him his particular kind of optimism in observing and recording both human and natural phenomena. It was his development of this view that sustained him after the collapse of his earlier political idealism as a result of his disillusion with rationalistic radicalism and with the course of the French Revolution. But the view, which nourished some of his best poetry, was based on moments of vision which occurred less frequently after 1805. In later years his increasing conservatism issued in a rhetorical moral poetry whose power is more diffused.

JENNI CALDER

'My heart leaps up'

My heart leaps up when I behold
 A rainbow in the sky:
So was it when my life began;
So is it now I am a man;
So be it when I shall grow old,
 Or let me die!
The Child is father of the Man;
And I could wish my days to be
Bound each to each by natural piety.

To a Butterfly

Stay near me – do not take thy flight!
A little longer stay in sight!
Much converse do I find in thee,
Historian of my infancy!
Float near me; do not yet depart!
Dead times revive in thee:
Thou bring'st, gay creature as thou art!
A solemn image to my heart,
My father's family!

Oh! pleasant, pleasant were the days,
The time, when in our childish plays,
My sister Emmeline and I
Together chased the butterfly!
A very hunter did I rush
Upon the prey; – with leaps and springs
I followed on from brake to bush;
But she, God love her! feared to brush
The dust from off its wings.

Alice Fell;

OR, POVERTY

The post-boy drove with fierce career,
For threatening clouds the moon had drowned;
When, as we hurried on, my ear
Was smitten with a startling sound.

As if the wind blew many ways,
I heard the sound, – and more and more;
It seemed to follow with the chaise,
And still I heard it as before.

At length I to the boy called out;
He stopped his horses at the word,
But neither cry, nor voice, nor shout,
Nor aught else like it, could be heard.

The boy then smacked his whip, and fast
The horses scampered through the rain;
But, hearing soon upon the blast
The cry, I bade him halt again.

Forthwith alighting on the ground,
'Whence comes,' said I, 'this piteous moan?'
And there a little Girl I found,
Sitting behind the chaise, alone.

'My cloak!' no other word she spake,
But loud and bitterly she wept,
As if her innocent heart would break;
And down from off her seat she leapt.

'What ails you, child?' – she sobbed, 'Look here!'
I saw it in the wheel entangled,
A weather-beaten rag as e'er
From any garden scare-crow dangled.

There, twisted between nave and spoke,
It hung, nor could at once be freed;
But our joint pains unloosed the cloak,
A miserable rag indeed!

'And whither are you going, child,
To-night along these lonesome ways?'
'To Durham,' answered she, half wild –
'Then come with me into the chaise.'

Insensible to all relief
Sat the poor girl, and forth did send
Sob after sob, as if her grief
Could never, never have an end.

'My child, in Durham do you dwell?'
She checked herself in her distress,
And said, 'My name is Alice Fell;
I'm fatherless and motherless.

'And I to Durham, Sir, belong.'
Again, as if the thought would choke
Her very heart, her grief grew strong;
And all was for her tattered cloak!

The chaise drove on; our journey's end
Was nigh; and, sitting by my side,
As if she had lost her only friend
She wept, nor would be pacified.

Up to the tavern-door we post;
Of Alice and her grief I told;
And I gave money to the host,
To buy a new cloak for the old.

'And let it be of duffil grey,
As warm a cloak as man can sell!'
Proud creature was she the next day,
The little orphan, Alice Fell!

Lucy Gray;

OR, SOLITUDE

Oft I had heard of Lucy Gray:
And, when I crossed the wild,
I chanced to see at break of day
The solitary child.

No mate, no comrade Lucy knew;
She dwelt on a wide moor,
– The sweetest thing that ever grew
Beside a human door!

You yet may spy the fawn at play,
The hare upon the green;
But the sweet face of Lucy Gray
Will never more be seen.

'To-night will be a stormy night –
You to the town must go;
And take a lantern, Child, to light
Your mother through the snow.'

'That, Father! will I gladly do:
'Tis scarcely afternoon –
The minster-clock has just struck two,
And yonder is the moon!'

At this the Father raised his hook,
And snapped a faggot-band;
He plied his work; – and Lucy took
The lantern in her hand.

Not blither is the mountain roe:
With many a wanton stroke
Her feet disperse the powdery snow,
That rises up like smoke.

The storm came on before its time;
She wandered up and down;
And many a hill did Lucy climb:
But never reached the town.

The wretched parents all that night
Went shouting far and wide;
But there was neither sound nor sight
To serve them for a guide.

At day-break on a hill they stood
That overlooked the moor;
And thence they saw the bridge of wood,
A furlong from their door.

They wept – and, turning homeward, cried,
'In heaven we all shall meet;'
– When in the snow the mother spied
The print of Lucy's feet.

Then downwards from the steep hill's edge
They tracked the footmarks small;
And through the broken hawthorn hedge,
And by the long stone-wall;

And then an open field they crossed:
The marks were still the same;
They tracked them on, nor ever lost;
And to the bridge they came.

They followed from the snowy bank
Those footmarks, one by one,
Into the middle of the plank;
And further there were none!

– Yet some maintain that to this day
She is a living child;
That you may see sweet Lucy Gray
Upon the lonesome wild.

O'er rough and smooth she trips along,
And never looks behind;
And sings a solitary song
That whistles in the wind.

We are seven

– – A simple Child,
That lightly draws its breath,
And feels its life in every limb,
What should it know of death?

I met a little cottage Girl:
She was eight years old, she said;
Her hair was thick with many a curl
That clustered round her head.

She had a rustic, woodland air,
And she was wildly clad:
Her eyes were fair, and very fair;
– Her beauty made me glad.

'Sisters and brothers, little maid,
How many may you be?'
'How many? Seven in all,' she said,
And wondering looked at me.

'And where are they? I pray you tell.'
She answered, 'Seven are we;
And two of us at Conway dwell,
And two are gone to sea.

'Two of us in the church-yard lie,
My sister and my brother;
And, in the church-yard cottage, I
Dwell near them with my mother.'

'You say that two at Conway dwell,
And two are gone to sea,
Yet ye are seven! I pray you tell,
Sweet Maid, how this may be.'

Then did the little Maid reply,
'Seven boys and girls are we;
Two of us in the church-yard lie,
Beneath the church-yard tree.'

'You run about, my little Maid,
Your limbs they are alive;
If two are in the church-yard laid,
Then ye are only five.'

'Their graves are green, they may be seen,'
The little Maid replied,
'Twelve steps or more from my mother's door,
And they are side by side.

'My stockings there I often knit,
My kerchief there I hem;
And there upon the ground I sit,
And sing a song to them.

'And often after sun-set, Sir,
When it is light and fair,
I take my little porringer,
And eat my supper there.

'The first that died was sister Jane;
In bed she moaning lay,
Till God released her of her pain;
And then she went away.

'So in the church-yard she was laid;
And, when the grass was dry,
Together round her grave we played,
My brother John and I.

'And when the ground was white with snow
And I could run and slide,
My brother John was forced to go,
And he lies by her side.'

'How many are you, then,' said I,
'If they two are in heaven?'
Quick was the little Maid's reply,
'O Master! we are seven.'

'But they are dead; those two are dead!
Their spirits are in heaven!'
'Twas throwing words away; for still
The little Maid would have her will,
And said, 'Nay, we are seven!'

To H. C.

SIX YEARS OLD

O thou! whose fancies from afar are brought;
Who of thy words dost make a mock apparel,
And fittest to unutterable thought
The breeze-like motion and the self-born carol;
Thou faery voyager! that dost float
In such clear water, that thy boat
May rather seem
To brood on air than on an earthly stream;
Suspended in a stream as clear as sky,
Where earth and heaven do make one imagery;
O blessed vision! happy child!
Thou art so exquisitely wild,
I think of thee with many fears
For what may be thy lot in future years.

I thought of times when Pain might be thy guest,
Lord of thy house and hospitality;
And Grief, uneasy lover! never rest
But when she sate within the touch of thee.
O too industrious folly!
O vain and causeless melancholy!
Nature will either end thee quite;
Or, lengthening out thy season of delight,
Preserve for thee, by individual right,
A young lamb's heart among the full-grown flocks.
What hast thou to do with sorrow,
Or the injuries of to-morrow?
Thou art a dew-drop, which the morn brings forth,
Ill fitted to sustain unkindly shocks,
Or to be trailed along the soiling earth;
A gem that glitters while it lives,
And no forewarning gives;
But, at the touch of wrong, without a strife
Slips in a moment out of life.

Elegiac Stanzas

SUGGESTED BY A PICTURE OF PEELE CASTLE, IN A
STORM, PAINTED BY SIR GEORGE BEAUMONT ·

I was thy neighbour once, thou rugged Pile!
Four summer weeks I dwelt in sight of thee:
I saw thee every day; and all the while
Thy Form was sleeping on a glassy sea.

So pure the sky, so quiet was the air!
So like, so very like, was day to day!
Whene'er I looked, thy Image still was there;
It trembled, but it never passed away.

How perfect was the calm! it seemed no sleep;
No mood, which season takes away, or brings:
I could have fancied that the mighty Deep
Was even the gentlest of all gentle Things.

Ah! then, if mine had been the Painter's hand,
To express what then I saw; and add the gleam,
The light that never was, on sea or land,
The consecration, and the Poet's dream;

I would have planted thee, thou hoary Pile
Amid a world how different from this!
Beside a sea that could not cease to smile;
On tranquil land, beneath a sky of bliss.

Thou shouldst have seemed a treasure-house divine
Of peaceful years; a chronicle of heaven; —
Of all the sunbeams that did ever shine
The very sweetest had to thee been given.

A Picture had it been of lasting ease,
Elysian quiet, without toil or strife;
No motion but the moving tide, a breeze,
Or merely silent Nature's breathing life.

Such, in the fond illusion of my heart,
Such Picture would I at that time have made:
And seen the soul of truth in every part,
A steadfast peace that might not be betrayed.

So once it would have been, – 'tis so no more;
I have submitted to a new control:
A power is gone, which nothing can restore;
A deep distress hath humanised my Soul.

Not for a moment could I now behold
A smiling sea, and be what I have been:
The feeling of my loss will ne'er be old;
This, which I know, I speak with mind serene.

Then, Beaumont, Friend! who would have been the Friend,
If he had lived, of Him whom I deplore,
This work of thine I blame not, but commend;
This sea in anger, and that dismal shore.

O 'tis a passionate Work! – yet wise and well,
Well chosen in the spirit that is here;
That Hulk which labours in the deadly swell,
This rueful sky, this pageantry of fear!

And this huge Castle, standing here sublime,
I love to see the look with which it braves,
Cased in the unfeeling armour of old time,
The lightning, the fierce wind, and trampling waves.

Farewell, farewell the heart that lives alone,
Housed in a dream, at distance from the Kind!
Such happiness, wherever it be known,
Is to be pitied; for 'tis surely blind.

But welcome fortitude, and patient cheer,
And frequent sights of what is to be borne!
Such sights, or worse, as are before me here. –
Not without hope we suffer and we mourn.

The 'Lucy' Poems

Strange fits of passion have I known:
And I will dare to tell,
But in the Lover's ear alone,
What once to me befell.

When she I loved looked every day
Fresh as a rose in June,
I to her cottage bent my way,
Beneath an evening-moon.

Upon the moon I fixed my eye,
All over the wide lea;
With quickening pace my horse drew nigh
Those paths so dear to me.

And now we reached the orchard-plot;
And, as we climbed the hill,
The sinking moon to Lucy's cot
Came near, and nearer still.

In one of those sweet dreams I slept,
Kind Nature's gentlest boon!
And all the while my eyes I kept
On the descending moon.

My horse moved on; hoof after hoof
He raised, and never stopped:
When down behind the cottage roof,
At once, the bright moon dropped.

What fond and wayward thoughts will slide
Into a Lover's head!
'O mercy!' to myself I cried,
'If Lucy should be dead!'

*

She dwelt among the untrodden ways
    Beside the springs of Dove,
A Maid whom there were none to praise
    And very few to love:

A violet by a mossy stone
    Half hidden from the eye!
— Fair as a star, when only one
    Is shining in the sky.

She lived unknown, and few could know
    When Lucy ceased to be;
But she is in her grave, and, oh,
    The difference to me!

*

I travelled among unknown men,
    In lands beyond the sea;
Nor, England! did I know till then
    What love I bore to thee.

'Tis past, that melancholy dream!
    Nor will I quit thy shore
A second time; for still I seem
    To love thee more and more.

Among thy mountains did I feel
   The joy of my desire;
And she I cherished turned her wheel
   Beside an English fire.

Thy mornings showed, thy nights concealed,
   The bowers where Lucy played;
And thine too is the last green field
   That Lucy's eyes surveyed.

*

Three years she grew in sun and shower,
Then Nature said, 'A lovelier flower
On earth was never sown;
This Child I to myself will take;
She shall be mine, and I will make
A Lady of my own.

'Myself will to my darling be
Both law and impulse: and with me
The Girl, in rock and plain,
In earth and heaven, in glade and bower,
Shall feel an overseeing power
To kindle or restrain.

'She shall be sportive as the fawn
That wild with glee across the lawn
Or up the mountain springs;
And hers shall be the breathing balm,
And hers the silence and the calm
Of mute insensate things.

'The floating clouds their state shall lend
To her; for her the willow bend;
Nor shall she fail to see

Even in the motions of the Storm
Grace that shall mould the Maiden's form
By silent sympathy.

'The stars of midnight shall be dear
To her; and she shall lean her ear
In many a secret place
Where rivulets dance their wayward round,
And beauty born of murmuring sound
Shall pass into her face.

'And vital feelings of delight
Shall rear her form to stately height,
Her virgin bosom swell;
Such thoughts to Lucy I will give
While she and I together live
Here in this happy dell.'

Thus Nature spake – The work was done –
How soon my Lucy's race was run!
She died, and left to me
This heath, this calm, and quiet scene;
The memory of what has been,
And never more will be.

*

A slumber did my spirit seal;
    I had no human fears:
She seemed a thing that could not feel
    The touch of earthly years.

No motion has she now, no force;
    She neither hears nor sees;
Rolled round in earth's diurnal course,
    With rocks, and stones, and trees.

The Green Linnet

Beneath these fruit-tree boughs that shed
Their snow-white blossoms on my head,
With brightest sunshine round me spread
    Of spring's unclouded weather,
In this sequestered nook how sweet
To sit upon my orchard-seat!
And birds and flowers once more to greet,
    My last year's friends together.

One have I marked, the happiest guest
In all this covert of the blest:
Hail to Thee, far above the rest
    In joy of voice and pinion!
Thou, Linnet! in thy green array,
Presiding Spirit here to-day,
Dost lead the revels of the May;
    And this is thy dominion.

While birds, and butterflies, and flowers,
Make all one band of paramours,
Thou, ranging up and down the bowers,
    Art sole in thy employment:
A Life, a Presence like the Air,
Scattering thy gladness without care,
Too blest with any one to pair:
    Thyself thy own enjoyment.

Amid yon tuft of hazel trees,
That twinkle to the gusty breeze,
Behold him perched in ecstasies,
    Yet seeming still to hover;
There! where the flutter of his wings
Upon his back and body flings
Shadows and sunny glimmerings,
    That cover him all over.

My dazzled sight he oft deceives,
A Brother of the dancing leaves;
Then flits, and from the cottage eaves
    Pours forth his song in gushes;
As if by that exulting strain
He mocked and treated with disdain
The voiceless Form he chose to feign,
    While fluttering in the bushes.

To the small Celandine

Pansies, lilies, kingcups, daisies,
Let them live upon their praises;
Long as there's a sun that sets,
Primroses will have their glory;
Long as there are violets,
They will have a place in story:
There's a flower that shall be mine,
'Tis the little Celandine.

Eyes of some men travel far
For the finding of a star;
Up and down the heavens they go,
Men that keep a mighty rout!
I'm as great as they, I trow,
Since the day I found thee out,
Little Flower – I'll make a stir,
Like a sage astronomer.

Modest, yet withal an Elf
Bold, and lavish of thyself;
Since we needs must first have met
I have seen thee, high and low,
Thirty years or more, and yet
'Twas a face I did not know;
Thou hast now, go where I may,
Fifty greetings in a day.

Ere a leaf is on a bush
In the time before the thrush
Has a thought about her nest,
Thou wilt come with half a call,
Spreading out thy glossy breast
Like a careless Prodigal;
Telling tales about the sun,
When we've little warmth, or none.

Poets, vain men in their mood!
Travel with the multitude:
Never heed them; I aver
That they all are wanton wooers;
But the thrifty cottager,
Who stirs little out of doors,
Joys to spy thee near her home;
Spring is coming, Thou art come!

Comfort have thou of thy merit,
Kindly, unassuming Spirit!
Careless of thy neighbourhood,
Thou dost show thy pleasant face
On the moor, and in the wood,
In the lane; – there's not a place,
Howsoever mean it be,
But 'tis good enough for thee.

Ill befall the yellow flowers,
Children of the flaring hours!
Buttercups, that will be seen,
Whether we will see or no;
Others, too, of lofty mien;
They have done as worldlings do,
Taken praise that should be thine,
Little, humble Celandine.

Prophet of delight and mirth,
Ill-requited upon earth;
Herald of a mighty band,
Of a joyous train ensuing,
Serving at my heart's command,
Tasks that are no tasks renewing,
I will sing, as doth behove,
Hymns in praise of what I love!

The Seven Sisters;

OR, THE SOLITUDE OF BINNORIE

I

Seven Daughters had Lord Archibald,
All children of one mother:
You could not say in one short day
What love they bore each other.
A garland of seven lilies wrought!
Seven Sisters that together dwell;
But he, bold Knight as ever fought,
Their Father, took of them no thought,
He loved the wars so well.
Sing, mournfully, oh! mournfully,
The solitude of Binnorie!

II

Fresh blows the wind, a western wind,
And from the shores of Erin,
Across the wave, a Rover brave
To Binnorie is steering:
Right onward to the Scottish strand
The gallant ship is borne;
The warriors leap upon the land,
And hark! the Leader of the band
Hath blown his bugle horn.

Sing, mournfully, oh! mournfully,
The solitude of Binnorie.

III

Beside a grotto of their own,
With boughs above them closing,
The Seven are laid, and in the shade
They lie like fawns reposing.
But now, upstarting with affright
At noise of man and steed,
Away they fly to left, to right –
Of your fair household, Father-Knight,
Methinks you take small heed!
Sing, mournfully, oh! mournfully,
The solitude of Binnorie.

IV

Away the seven fair Campbells fly,
And over hill and hollow,
With menace proud, and insult loud,
The youthful Rovers follow.
Cried they, 'Your Father loves to roam:
Enough for him to find
The empty house when he comes home;
For us your yellow ringlets comb,
For us be fair and kind!'
Sing, mournfully, oh! mournfully,
The solitude of Binnorie.

V

Some close behind, some side by side,
Like clouds in stormy weather;
They run, and cry, 'Nay, let us die,
And let us die together.'

A lake was near; the shore was steep;
There never foot had been;
They ran, and with a desperate leap
Together plunged into the deep,
Nor ever more were seen.
Sing, mournfully, oh! mournfully,
The solitude of Binnorie.

VI

The stream that flows out of the lake,
As through the glen it rambles,
Repeats a moan o'er moss and stone,
For those seven lovely Campbells.
Seven little Islands, green and bare,
Have risen from out the deep:
The fishers say, those sisters fair
By faeries all are buried there,
And there together sleep.
Sing, mournfully, oh! mournfully,
The solitude of Binnorie.

To the Cuckoo

O blithe New-comer! I have heard,
I hear thee and rejoice.
O Cuckoo! shall I call thee Bird,
Or but a wandering Voice?

While I am lying on the grass
Thy twofold shout I hear;
From hill to hill it seems to pass
At once far off, and near.

Though babbling only to the Vale,
Of sunshine and of flowers,
Thou bringest unto me a tale
Of visionary hours.

Thrice welcome, darling of the Spring!
Even yet thou art to me
No bird, but an invisible thing,
A voice, a mystery;

The same whom in my schoolboy days
I listened to; that Cry
Which made me look a thousand ways
In bush, and tree, and sky.

To seek thee did I often rove
Through woods and on the green;
And thou wert still a hope, a love;
Still longed for, never seen.

And I can listen to thee yet;
Can lie upon the plain
And listen, till I do beget
That golden time again.

O blessed Bird! the earth we pace
Again appears to be
An unsubstantial, faery place;
That is fit home for Thee!

Nutting

———————————It seems a day
(I speak of one from many singled out)
One of those heavenly days that cannot die
When, in the eagerness of boyish hope,
I left our cottage-threshold, sallying forth
With a huge wallet o'er my shoulders slung,
A nutting-crook in hand; and turned my steps
Tow'rd some far-distant wood, a Figure quaint,
Tricked out in proud disguise of cast-off weeds
Which for that service had been husbanded,
By exhortation of my frugal Dame —
Motley accoutrement, of power to smile
At thorns, and brakes, and brambles, — and in truth
More ragged than need was! O'er pathless rocks,
Through beds of matted fern, and tangled thickets,
Forcing my way, I came to one dear nook
Unvisited, where not a broken bough
Drooped with its withered leaves, ungracious sign
Of devastation; but the hazels rose
Tall and erect, with tempting clusters hung,
A virgin scene! — A little while I stood,
Breathing with such suppression of the heart
As joy delights in; and with wise restraint
Voluptuous, fearless of a rival, eyed
The banquet; — or beneath the trees I sate
Among the flowers, and with the flowers I played;
A temper known to those who, after long
And weary expectation, have been blest
With sudden happiness beyond all hope.
Perhaps it was a bower beneath whose leaves
The violets of five seasons re-appear
And fade, unseen by any human eye;
Where fairy water-breaks do murmur on

For ever; and I saw the sparkling foam,
And – with my cheek on one of those green stones
That, fleeced with moss, under the shady trees,
Lay round me, scattered like a flock of sheep –
I heard the murmur and the murmuring sound,
In that sweet mood when pleasure loves to pay
Tribute to ease; and, of its joy secure,
The heart luxuriates with indifferent things,
Wasting its kindliness on stocks and stones,
And on the vacant air. Then up I rose,
And dragged to earth both branch and bough, with crash
And merciless ravage: and the shady nook
Of hazels, and the green and mossy bower,
Deformed and sullied, patiently gave up
Their quiet being: and unless I now
Confound my present feelings with the past,
Ere from the mutilated bower I turned
Exulting, rich beyond the wealth of kings,
I felt a sense of pain when I beheld
The silent trees, and saw the intruding sky. –
Then, dearest Maiden, move along these shades
In gentleness of heart; with gentle hand
Touch – for there is a spirit in the woods.

She was a Phantom of Delight

She was a Phantom of delight
When first she gleamed upon my sight;
A lovely Apparition, sent
To be a moment's ornament;
Her eyes as stars of Twilight fair;
Like Twilight's, too, her dusky hair;
But all things else about her drawn
From May-time and the cheerful Dawn;
A dancing Shape, an Image gay,
To haunt, to startle, and way-lay.

I saw her upon nearer view,
A Spirit, yet a Woman too!
Her household motions light and free,
And steps of virgin-liberty;
A countenance in which did meet
Sweet records, promises as sweet;
A Creature not too bright or good
For human nature's daily food;
For transient sorrows, simple wiles,
Praise, blame, love, kisses, tears, and smiles.

And now I see with eye serene
The very pulse of the machine;
A Being breathing thoughtful breath,
A Traveller between life and death;
The reason firm, the temperate will,
Endurance, foresight, strength, and skill;
A perfect Woman, nobly planned,
To warn, to comfort, and command;
And yet a Spirit still, and bright
With something of angelic light.

The Daffodils

I wandered lonely as a cloud
That floats on high o'er vales and hills,
When all at once I saw a crowd,
A host, of golden daffodils;
Beside the lake, beneath the trees,
Fluttering and dancing in the breeze.

Continuous as the stars that shine
And twinkle on the milky way,
They stretched in never-ending line
Along the margin of a bay:
Ten thousand saw I at a glance,
Tossing their heads in sprightly dance.

The waves beside them danced; but they
Out-did the sparkling waves in glee:
A poet could not but be gay,
In such a jocund company:
I gazed – and gazed – but little thought
What wealth the show to me had brought:

For oft, when on my couch I lie
In vacant or in pensive mood,
They flash upon that inward eye
Which is the bliss of solitude;
And then my heart with pleasure fills,
And dances with the daffodils.

The Reverie of Poor Susan

At the corner of Wood Street, when daylight appears,
Hangs a Thrush that sings loud, it has sung for three years:
Poor Susan has passed by the spot, and has heard
In the silence of morning the song of the Bird.

'Tis a note of enchantment; what ails her? She sees
A mountain ascending, a vision of trees;
Bright volumes of vapour through Lothbury glide,
And a river flows on through the vale of Cheapside.

Green pastures she views in the midst of the dale,
Down which she so often has tripped with her pail;
And a single small cottage, a nest like a dove's,
The one only dwelling on earth that she loves.

She looks, and her heart is in heaven: but they fade,
The mist and the river, the hill and the shade:
The stream will not flow, and the hill will not rise,
And the colours have all passed away from her eyes!

Lines

COMPOSED A FEW MILES ABOVE TINTERN ABBEY, ON
REVISITING THE BANKS OF THE WYE DURING A
TOUR. 13 JULY 1798.

Five years have past; five summers, with the length
Of five long winters! and again I hear
These waters, rolling from their mountain-springs
With a soft inland murmur. – Once again
Do I behold these steep and lofty cliffs,
That on a wild secluded scene impress
Thoughts of more deep seclusion; and connect
The landscape with the quiet of the sky.
The day is come when I again repose
Here, under this dark sycamore, and view
These plots of cottage-ground, these orchard-tufts,
Which at this season, with their unripe fruits,
Are clad in one green hue, and lose themselves
'Mid groves and copses. Once again I see
These hedge-rows, hardly hedge-rows, little lines
Of sportive wood run wild: these pastoral farms,
Green to the very door; and wreaths of smoke
Sent up, in silence, from among the trees!
With some uncertain notice, as might seem
Of vagrant dwellers in the houseless woods,
Or of some Hermit's cave, where by his fire
The Hermit sits alone.
                            These beauteous forms,
Through a long absence, have not been to me
As is a landscape to a blind man's eye:
But oft, in lonely rooms, and 'mid the din
Of towns and cities, I have owed to them,
In hours of weariness, sensations sweet,
Felt in the blood, and felt along the heart;

And passing even into my purer mind,
With tranquil restoration: — feelings too
Of unremembered pleasure: such, perhaps,
As have no slight or trivial influence
On that best portion of a good man's life,
His little, nameless, unremembered, acts
Of kindness and of love. Nor less, I trust,
To them I may have owed another gift,
Of aspect more sublime; that blessed mood,
In which the burthen of the mystery,
In which the heavy and the weary weight
Of all this unintelligible world,
Is lightened: — that serene and blessed mood,
In which the affections gently lead us on, —
Until, the breath of this corporeal frame
And even the motion of our human blood
Almost suspended, we are laid asleep
In body, and become a living soul:
While with an eye made quiet by the power
Of harmony, and the deep power of joy,
We see into the life of things.
                              If this
Be but a vain belief, yet, oh! how oft —
In darkness and amid the many shapes
Of joyless daylight; when the fretful stir
Unprofitable, and the fever of the world,
Have hung upon the beatings of my heart —
How oft, in spirit, have I turned to thee,
O sylvan Wye! thou wanderer thro' the woods,
How often has my spirit turned to thee!

   And now, with gleams of half-extinguished thought,
With many recognitions dim and faint,
And somewhat of a sad perplexity,
The picture of the mind revives again:
While here I stand, not only with the sense
Of present pleasure, but with pleasing thoughts

That in this moment there is life and food
For future years. And so I dare to hope,
Though changed, no doubt, from what I was when first
I came among these hills; when like a roe
I bounded o'er the mountains, by the sides
Of the deep rivers, and the lonely streams,
Wherever nature led: more like a man
Flying from something that he dreads than one
Who sought the thing he loved. For nature then
(The coarser pleasures of my boyish days,
And their glad animal movements all gone by)
To me was all in all. – I cannot paint
What then I was. The sounding cataract
Haunted me like a passion: the tall rock,
The mountain, and the deep and gloomy wood,
Their colours and their forms, were then to me
An appetite; a feeling and a love,
That had no need of a remoter charm,
By thought supplied, nor any interest
Unborrowed from the eye. – That time is past,
And all its aching joys are now no more,
And all its dizzy raptures. Not for this
Faint I, nor mourn nor murmur; other gifts
Have followed; for such loss, I would believe,
Abundant recompense. For I have learned
To look on nature, not as in the hour
Of thoughtless youth; but hearing oftentimes
The still, sad music of humanity,
Nor harsh nor grating, though of ample power
To chasten and subdue. And I have felt
A presence that disturbs me with the joy
Of elevated thoughts; a sense sublime
Of something far more deeply interfused,
Whose dwelling is the light of setting suns,
And the round ocean and the living air,
And the blue sky, and in the mind of man:
A motion and a spirit, that impels

All thinking things, all objects of all thought,
And rolls through all things. Therefore am I still
A lover of the meadows and the woods,
And mountains; and of all that we behold
From this green earth; of all the mighty world
Of eye, and ear, – both what they half create,
And what perceive; well pleased to recognise
In nature and the language of the sense
The anchor of my purest thoughts, the nurse,
The guide, the guardian of my heart, and soul
Of all my moral being.
                                    Nor perchance,
If I were not thus taught, should I the more
Suffer my genial spirits to decay:
For thou art with me here upon the banks
Of this fair river; thou my dearest Friend,
My dear, dear Friend; and in thy voice I catch
The language of my former heart, and read
My former pleasures in the shooting lights
Of thy wild eyes. Oh! yet a little while
May I behold in thee what I was once,
My dear, dear Sister! and this prayer I make,
Knowing that Nature never did betray
The heart that loved her; 'tis her privilege,
Through all the years of this our life, to lead
From joy to joy: for she can so inform
The mind that is within us, so impress
With quietness and beauty, and so feed
With lofty thoughts, that neither evil tongues,
Rash judgements, nor the sneers of selfish men,
Nor greetings where no kindness is, nor all
The dreary intercourse of daily life,
Shall e'er prevail against us, or disturb
Our cheerful faith, that all which we behold
Is full of blessings. Therefore let the moon
Shine on thee in thy solitary walk;
And let the misty mountain-winds be free

To blow against thee: and, in after years,
When these wild ecstasies shall be matured
Into a sober pleasure; when thy mind
Shall be a mansion for all lovely forms,
Thy memory be as a dwelling-place
For all sweet sounds and harmonies; oh! then,
If solitude, or fear, or pain, or grief,
Should be thy portion, with what healing thoughts
Of tender joy wilt thou remember me,
And these my exhortations! Nor, perchance –
If I should be where I no more can hear
Thy voice, nor catch from thy wild eyes these gleams
Of past existence – wilt thou then forget
That on the banks of this delightful stream
We stood together; and that I, so long
A worshipper of Nature, hither came
Unwearied in that service: rather say
With warmer love – oh! with far deeper zeal
Of holier love. Nor wilt thou then forget
That after many wanderings, many years
Of absence, these steep woods and lofty cliffs,
And this green pastoral landscape, were to me
More dear, both for themselves and for thy sake!

Expostulation and Reply

'Why, William, on that old grey stone,
Thus for the length of half a day,
Why, William, sit you thus alone,
And dream your time away?

'Where are your books? – that light bequeathed
To Beings else forlorn and blind!
Up! up! and drink the spirit breathed
From dead men to their kind.

'You look round on your Mother Earth,
As if she for no purpose bore you;
As if you were her first-born birth,
And none had lived before you!'

One morning thus, by Esthwaite lake,
When life was sweet, I knew not why,
To me my good friend Matthew spake,
And thus I made reply:

'The eye – it cannot choose but see;
We cannot bid the ear be still;
Our bodies feel, where'er they be,
Against or with our will.

'Nor less I deem that there are Powers
Which of themselves our minds impress;
That we can feed this mind of ours
In a wise passiveness.

'Think you, 'mid all this mighty sum
Of things for ever speaking,
That nothing of itself will come,
But we must still be seeking?

' – Then ask not wherefore, here, alone,
Conversing as I may,
I sit upon this old grey stone,
And dream my time away.'

The Tables Turned

Up! up! my Friend, and quit your books;
   Or surely you'll grow double:
Up! up! my Friend, and clear your looks;
   Why all this toil and trouble?

The sun, above the mountain's head,
    A freshening lustre mellow
Through all the long green fields has spread
    His first sweet evening yellow.

Books! 'tis a dull and endless strife:
    Come, hear the woodland linnet,
How sweet his music! on my life,
    There's more of wisdom in it.

And hark! how blithe the throstle sings!
    He, too, is no mean preacher:
Come forth into the light of things,
    Let Nature be your Teacher.

She has a world of ready wealth,
    Our minds and hearts to bless —
Spontaneous wisdom breathed by health,
    Truth breathed by cheerfulness.

One impulse from a vernal wood
    May teach you more of man,
Of moral evil and of good,
    Than all the sages can.

Sweet is the lore which Nature brings;
    Our meddling intellect
Mis-shapes the beauteous forms of things: —
    We murder to dissect.

Enough of Science and of Art;
    Close up those barren leaves;
Come forth, and bring with you a heart
    That watches and receives.

To a Young Lady,

WHO HAD BEEN REPROACHED FOR TAKING
LONG WALKS IN THE COUNTRY

Dear Child of Nature, let them rail!
– There is a nest in a green dale,
A harbour and a hold;
Where thou, a Wife and Friend, shalt see
Thy own heart-stirring days, and be
A light to young and old.

There, healthy as a shepherd boy,
And treading among flowers of joy
Which at no season fade,
Thou, while thy babes around thee cling,
Shalt show us how divine a thing
A Woman may be made.

Thy thoughts and feelings shall not die,
Nor leave thee, when grey hairs are nigh,
A melancholy slave;
But an old age serene and bright,
And lovely as a Lapland night,
Shall lead thee to thy grave.

Vernal Ode

I

Beneath the concave of an April sky,
When all the fields with freshest green were dight,
Appeared, in presence of the spiritual eye
That aids or supersedes our grosser sight,
The form and rich habiliments of One
Whose countenance bore resemblance to the sun,

When it reveals, in evening majesty,
Features half lost amid their own pure light.
Poised like a weary cloud, in middle air
He hung, – then floated with angelic ease
(Softening that bright effulgence by degrees)
Till he had reached a summit sharp and bare,
Where oft the venturous heifer drinks the noontide breeze.
Upon the apex of that lofty cone
Alighted, there the Stranger stood alone;
Fair as a gorgeous Fabric of the east
Suddenly raised by some enchanter's power,
Where nothing was; and firm as some old Tower
Of Britain's realm, whose leafy crest
Waves high, embellished by a gleaming shower

II

Beneath the shadow of his purple wings
Rested a golden harp; – he touched the strings
And, after prelude of unearthly sound
Poured through the echoing hills around,
He sang –
            'No wintry desolations,
Scorching blight or noxious dew,
Affect my native habitations;
Buried in glory, far beyond the scope
Of man's enquiring gaze, but to his hope
Imaged, though faintly, in the hue
Profound of night's ethereal blue;
And in the aspect of each radiant orb; –
Some fixed, some wandering with no timid curb;
But wandering star and fixed, to mortal eye,
Blended in absolute serenity,
And free from semblance of decline; –
Fresh as if Evening brought their natal hour,
Her darkness splendour gave, her silence power,
To testify of Love and Grace divine.

III

'What if those bright fires
Shine subject to decay,
Sons haply of extinguished sires,
Themselves to lose their light, or pass away
Like clouds before the wind,
Be thanks poured out to Him whose hand bestows,
Nightly, on human kind
That vision of endurance and repose.
– And though to every draught of vital breath,
Renewed throughout the bounds of earth or ocean,
The melancholy gates of Death
Respond with sympathetic motion;
Though all that feeds on nether air
Howe'er magnificent or fair,
Grows but to perish, and entrust
Its ruins to their kindred dust;
Yet, by the Almighty's ever-during care,
Her procreant vigils Nature keeps
Amid the unfathomable deeps;
And saves the peopled fields of earth
From dread of emptiness or dearth.
Thus, in their stations, lifting tow'rd the sky
The foliaged head in cloud-like majesty,
The shadow-casting race of trees survive:
Thus, in the train of Spring, arrive
Sweet flowers; – what living eye hath viewed
Their myriads? – endlessly renewed,
Wherever strikes the sun's glad ray;
Where'er the subtle waters stray;
Wherever sportive breezes bend
Their course, or genial showers descend!
Mortals, rejoice! the very Angels quit
Their mansions unsusceptible of change,
Amid your pleasant bowers to sit,
And through your sweet vicissitudes to range!'

IV

O, nursed at happy distance from the cares
Of a too-anxious world, mild pastoral Muse!
That to the sparkling crown Urania wears,
And to her sister Clio's laurel wreath,
Preferr'st a garland culled from purple heath,
Or blooming thicket moist with morning dews;
Was such bright Spectacle vouchsafed to me?
And was it granted to the simple ear
Of thy contented Votary
Such melody to hear!
Him rather suits it, side by side with thee,
Wrapped in a fit of pleasing indolence,
While thy tired lute hangs on the hawthorn-tree,
To lie and listen – till o'er-drowsèd sense
Sinks, hardly conscious of the influence –
To the soft murmur of the vagrant Bee.
– A slender sound! yet hoary Time
Doth to the *Soul* exalt it with the chime
Of all his years; – a company
Of ages coming, ages gone;
(Nations from before them sweeping,
Regions in destruction steeping,)
But every awful note in unison
With that faint utterance, which tells
Of treasure sucked from buds and bells,
For the pure keeping of those waxen cells;
Where She – a statist prudent to confer
Upon the common weal; a warrior bold,
Radiant all over with unburnished gold,
And armed with living spear for mortal fight;
        A cunning forager
That spreads no waste; a social builder; one
In whom all busy offices unite
With all fine functions that afford delight –
Safe through the winter storms in quiet dwells!

V

And is She brought within the power
Of vision? – o'er this tempting flower
Hovering until the petals stay
Her flight, and take its voice away! –
Observe each wing! – a tiny van!
The structure of her laden thigh,
How fragile! yet of ancestry
Mysteriously remote and high;
High as the imperial front of man;
The roseate bloom on woman's cheek;
The soaring eagle's curvèd beak;
The white plumes of the floating swan;
Old as the tiger's paw, the lion's mane
Ere shaken by that mood of stern disdain
At which the desert trembles. – Humming Bee!
Thy sting was needless then, perchance unknown,
The seeds of malice were not sown;
All creatures met in peace, from fierceness free,
And no pride blended with their dignity.
– Tears had not broken from their source;
Nor Anguish strayed from her Tartarean den;
The golden years maintained a course
Not undiversified though smooth and even;
We were not mocked with glimpse and shadow then,
Bright Seraphs mixed familiarly with men;
And earth and stars composed a universal heaven!

It is a beauteous evening

It is a beauteous evening, calm and free,
The holy time is quiet as a Nun
Breathless with adoration; the broad sun
Is sinking down in its tranquillity;
The gentleness of heaven broods o'er the Sea:
Listen! the mighty Being is awake,
And doth with his eternal motion make
A sound like thunder – everlastingly.
Dear Child! dear Girl! that walkest with me here,
If thou appear untouched by solemn thought,
Thy nature is not therefore less divine:
Thou liest in Abraham's bosom all the year;
And worshipp'st at the Temple's inner shrine,
God being with thee when we know it not.

The world is too much with us

The world is too much with us; late and soon,
Getting and spending, we lay waste our powers:
Little we see in Nature that is ours;
We have given our hearts away, a sordid boon!
This Sea that bares her bosom to the moon;
The winds that will be howling at all hours,
And are up-gathered now like sleeping flowers;
For this, for everything, we are out of tune;
It moves us not. – Great God! I'd rather be
A Pagan suckled in a creed outworn;
So might I, standing on this pleasant lea,
Have glimpses that would make me less forlorn;
Have sight of Proteus rising from the sea;
Or hear old Triton blow his wreathèd horn.

Scorn not the Sonnet

Scorn not the Sonnet; Critic, you have frowned,
Mindless of its just honours; with this key
Shakespeare unlocked his heart; the melody
Of this small lute gave ease to Petrarch's wound;
A thousand times this pipe did Tasso sound;
With it Camöens soothed an exile's grief;
The Sonnet glittered a gay myrtle leaf
Amid the cypress with which Dante crowned
His visionary brow: a glow-worm lamp,
It cheered mild Spenser, called from Faery-land
To struggle through dark ways; and when a damp
Fell round the path of Milton, in his hand
The Thing became a trumpet; whence he blew
Soul-animating strains – alas, too few!

With how sad steps, O Moon

'With how sad steps, O Moon, thou climb'st the sky,
How silently, and with how wan a face!'*
Where art thou? Thou so often seen on high
Running among the clouds a Wood-nymph's race!
Unhappy Nuns, whose common breath's a sigh
Which they would stifle, move at such a pace!
The northern Wind, to call thee to the chase,
Must blow to-night his bugle horn. Had I
The power of Merlin, Goddess! this should be:
And all the stars, fast as the clouds were riven,
Should sally forth, to keep thee company,
Hurrying and sparkling through the clear blue heaven;
But, Cynthia! should to thee the palm be given,
Queen both for beauty and for majesty.

*Quoted from Sir Philip Sidney's sonnet.

Composed upon Westminster Bridge

Earth has not anything to show more fair:
Dull would he be of soul who could pass by
A sight so touching in its majesty:
This City now doth, like a garment, wear
The beauty of the morning; silent, bare,
Ships, towers, domes, theatres, and temples lie
Open unto the fields, and to the sky;
All bright and glittering in the smokeless air.
Never did sun more beautifully steep
In his first splendour, valley, rock, or hill;
Ne'er saw I, never felt, a calm so deep!
The river glideth at his own sweet will:
Dear God! the very houses seem asleep;
And all that mighty heart is lying still!

On the Extinction of the Venetian Republic

Once did She hold the gorgeous east in fee;
And was the safeguard of the west: the worth
Of Venice did not fall below her birth,
Venice, the eldest Child of Liberty.
She was a maiden City, bright and free;
No guile seduced, no force could violate;
And, when she took unto herself a Mate,
She must espouse the everlasting Sea.
And what if she had seen those glories fade,
Those titles vanish, and that strength decay;
Yet shall some tribute of regret be paid
When her long life hath reached its final day:
Men are we, and must grieve when even the Shade
Of that which once was great is passed away.

Thought of a Briton on the Subjugation of Switzerland

Two Voices are there; one is of the sea,
One of the mountains; each a mighty Voice:
In both from age to age thou didst rejoice,
They were thy chosen music, Liberty!
There came a Tyrant, and with holy glee
Thou fought'st against him; but hast vainly striven:
Thou from thy Alpine holds at length art driven,
Where not a torrent murmurs heard by thee.
Of one deep bliss thine ear hath been bereft:
Then cleave, O cleave to that which still is left;
For, high-souled Maid, what sorrow would it be
That Mountain floods should thunder as before,
And Ocean bellow from his rocky shore,
And neither awful Voice be heard by thee!

Milton

Milton! thou shouldst be living at this hour:
England hath need of thee: she is a fen
Of stagnant waters: altar, sword, and pen,
Fireside, the heroic wealth of hall and bower,
Have forfeited their ancient English dower
Of inward happiness. We are selfish men;
Oh! raise us up, return to us again;
And give us manners, virtue, freedom, power.
Thy soul was like a Star, and dwelt apart;
Thou hadst a voice whose sound was like the sea:
Pure as the naked heavens, majestic, free,
So didst thou travel on life's common way,
In cheerful godliness; and yet thy heart
The lowliest duties on herself did lay.

To the Men of Kent. October, 1803

Vanguard of Liberty, ye men of Kent,
Ye children of a Soil that doth advance
Her haughty brow against the coast of France,
Now is the time to prove your hardiment!
To France be words of invitation sent!
They from their fields can see the countenance
Of your fierce war, may ken the glittering lance,
And hear you shouting forth your brave intent.
Left single, in bold parley, ye, of yore,
Did from the Norman win a gallant wreath;
Confirmed the charters that were yours before; –
No parleying now. In Britain is one breath;
We all are with you now from shore to shore; –
Ye men of Kent, 'tis victory or death!

The Solitary Reaper

Behold her, single in the field,
Yon solitary Highland Lass!
Reaping and singing by herself;
Stop here, or gently pass!
Alone she cuts and binds the grain,
And sings a melancholy strain;
O listen! for the Vale profound
Is overflowing with the sound.

No Nightingale did ever chaunt
More welcome notes to weary bands
Of travellers in some shady haunt,
Among Arabian sands:

A voice so thrilling ne'er was heard
In spring-time from the Cuckoo-bird,
Breaking the silence of the seas
Among the farthest Hebrides.

Will no one tell me what she sings? –
Perhaps the plaintive numbers flow
For old, unhappy, far-off things,
And battles long ago:
Or is it some more humble lay,
Familiar matter of to-day?
Some natural sorrow, loss, or pain,
That has been, and may be again?

Whate'er the theme, the Maiden sang
As if her song could have no ending;
I saw her singing at her work,
And o'er the sickle bending; –
I listened, motionless and still;
And, as I mounted up the hill,
The music in my heart I bore,
Long after it was heard no more.

Yarrow Unvisited

From Stirling castle we had seen
The mazy Forth unravelled;
Had trod the banks of Clyde, and Tay,
And with the Tweed had travelled;
And when we came to Clovenford,
Then said my '*winsome Marrow*',
'Whate'er betide, we'll turn aside,
And see the Braes of Yarrow.'

'Let Yarrow folk, frae Selkirk town,
Who have been buying, selling,
Go back to Yarrow, 'tis their own;
Each maiden to her dwelling!
On Yarrow's banks let herons feed,
Hares couch, and rabbits burrow!
But we will downward with the Tweed,
Not turn aside to Yarrow.

'There's Galla Water, Leader Haughs,
Both lying right before us;
And Dryborough, where with chiming Tweed
The lintwhites sing in chorus;
There's pleasant Tiviot-dale, a land
Made blithe with plough and harrow:
Why throw away a needful day
To go in search of Yarrow?

'What's Yarrow but a river bare,
That glides the dark hills under?
There are a thousand such elsewhere
As worthy of your wonder.'
– Strange words they seemed of slight and scorn;
My True-love sighed for sorrow;
And looked me in the face, to think
I thus could speak of Yarrow!

'Oh! green,' said I, 'are Yarrow's holms,
And sweet is Yarrow flowing!
Fair hangs the apple frae the rock,
But we will leave it growing.
O'er hilly path, and open Strath,
We'll wander Scotland thorough;
But, though so near, we will not turn
Into the dale of Yarrow.

'Let beeves and home-bred kine partake
The sweets of Burn-mill meadow;
The swan on still St Mary's Lake
Float double, swan and shadow!
We will not see them; will not go,
To-day, nor yet to-morrow;
Enough if in our hearts we know
There's such a place as Yarrow.

'Be Yarrow stream unseen, unknown!
It must, or we shall rue it:
We have a vision of our own;
Ah! why should we undo it?
The treasured dreams of times long past,
We'll keep them, winsome Marrow!
For when we're there, although 'tis fair,
'Twill be another Yarrow!

'If Care with freezing years should come,
And wandering seem but folly, –
Should we be loth to stir from home,
And yet be melancholy;
Should life be dull, and spirits low,
'Twill soothe us in our sorrow,
That earth hath something yet to show,
The bonny holms of Yarrow!'

Yarrow Visited

SEPTEMBER 1814

And is this – Yarrow? – *This* the Stream
Of which my fancy cherished,
So faithfully, a waking dream?
An image that hath perished!
O that some Minstrel's harp were near,
To utter notes of gladness,
And chase this silence from the air,
That fills my heart with sadness!

Yet why? – a silvery current flows
With uncontrolled meanderings;
Nor have these eyes by greener hills
Been soothed, in all my wanderings.
And, through her depths, Saint Mary's Lake
Is visibly delighted;
For not a feature of those hills
Is in the mirror slighted.

A blue sky bends o'er Yarrow vale,
Save where that pearly whiteness
Is round the rising sun diffused,
A tender hazy brightness;
Mild dawn of promise! that excludes
All profitless dejection:
Though not unwilling here to admit
A pensive recollection.

Where was it that the famous Flower
Of Yarrow Vale lay bleeding?
His bed perchance was yon smooth mound
On which the herd is feeding:

And haply from this crystal pool,
Now peaceful as the morning,
The Water-wraith ascended thrice –
And gave his doleful warning.

Delicious is the Lay that sings
The haunts of happy Lovers,
The path that leads them to the grove,
The leafy grove that covers:
And Pity sanctifies the Verse
That paints, by strength of sorrow,
The unquestionable strength of love;
Bear witness, rueful Yarrow!

But thou, that didst appear so fair
To fond imagination,
Dost rival in the light of day
Her delicate creation:
Meek loveliness is round thee spread,
A softness still and holy;
The grace of forest charms decayed,
And pastoral melancholy.

That region left, the vale unfolds
Rich groves of lofty stature,
With Yarrow winding through the pomp
Of cultivated nature;
And, rising from those lofty groves,
Behold a Ruin hoary!
The shattered front of Newark's Towers,
Renowned in Border story.

Fair scenes of childhood's opening bloom,
For sportive youth to stray in;
For manhood to enjoy his strength;
And age to wear away in!

Yon cottage seems a bower of bliss,
A covert for protection
Of tender thoughts, that nestle there –
The brood of chaste affection.

How sweet, on this autumnal day,
The wild-wood fruits to gather,
And on my True-love's forehead plant
A crest of blooming heather!
And what if I enwreathed my own!
'Twere no offence to reason;
The sober Hills thus deck their brows
To meet the wintry season.

I see – but not by sight alone,
Loved Yarrow, have I won thee;
A ray of fancy still survives –
Her sunshine plays upon thee!
Thy ever-youthful waters keep
A course of lively pleasure;
And gladsome notes my lips can breathe,
Accordant to the measure.

The vapours linger round the Heights,
They melt, and soon must vanish;
One hour is theirs, nor more is mine –
Sad thought, which I would banish,
But that I know, where'er I go,
Thy genuine image, Yarrow!
Will dwell with me – to heighten joy,
And cheer my mind in sorrow.

Yarrow Revisited

The following Stanzas are a memorial of a day passed with Sir Walter Scott and other Friends visiting the Banks of the Yarrow under his guidance immediately before his departure from Abbotsford, for Naples.

The gallant Youth, who may have gained,
    Or seeks, a 'winsome Marrow',
Was but an Infant in the lap
    When first I looked on Yarrow;
Once more, by Newark's Castle-gate
    Long left without a warder,
I stood, looked, listened, and with Thee,
    Great Minstrel of the Border!

Grave thoughts ruled wide on that sweet day,
    Their dignity installing
In gentle bosoms, while sere leaves
    Were on the bough, or falling;
But breezes played, and sunshine gleamed –
    The forest to embolden;
Reddened the fiery hues, and shot
    Transparence through the golden.

For busy thoughts the Stream flowed on
    In foamy agitation;
And slept in many a crystal pool
    For quiet contemplation:
No public and no private care
    The freeborn mind enthralling,
We made a day of happy hours,
    Our happy days recalling.

Brisk Youth appeared, the Morn of Youth,
    With freaks of graceful folly, –
Life's temperate Noon, her sober Eve,
    Her Night not melancholy;

Past, present, future, all appeared
  In harmony united,
Like guests that meet, and some from far,
  By cordial love invited.

And if, as Yarrow, through the woods
  And down the meadow ranging,
Did meet us with unaltered face,
  Though we were changed and changing;
If, *then*, some natural shadows spread
  Our inward prospect over,
The soul's deep valley was not slow
  Its brightness to recover.

Eternal blessings on the Muse,
  And her divine employment!
The blameless Muse, who trains her Sons
  For hope and calm enjoyment;
Albeit sickness, lingering yet,
  Has o'er their pillow brooded;
And Care waylays their steps – a Sprite
  Not easily eluded.

For thee, O Scott! compelled to change
  Green Eildon-hill and Cheviot
For warm Vesuvio's vine-clad slopes;
  And leave thy Tweed and Tiviot
For mild Sorento's breezy waves;
  May classic Fancy, linking
With native Fancy her fresh aid,
  Preserve thy heart from sinking!

Oh! while they minister to thee,
  Each vying with the other,
May Health return to mellow Age,
  With Strength, her venturous brother;

And Tiber, and each brook and rill
   Renowned in song and story,
With unimagined beauty shine,
   Nor lose one ray of glory!

For Thou, upon a hundred streams,
   By tales of love and sorrow,
Of faithful love, undaunted truth,
   Hast shed the power of Yarrow;
And streams unknown, hills yet unseen,
   Wherever they invite Thee,
At parent Nature's grateful call,
   With gladness must requite Thee.

A gracious welcome shall be thine,
   Such looks of love and honour
As thy own Yarrow gave to me,
   When first I gazed upon her;
Beheld what I had feared to see,
   Unwilling to surrender
Dreams treasured up from early days,
   The holy and the tender.

And what, for this frail world, were all
   That mortals do or suffer,
Did no responsive harp, no pen,
   Memorial tribute offer?
Yea, what were mighty Nature's self?
   Her features, could they win us,
Unhelped by the poetic voice
   That hourly speaks within us?

Nor deem that localised Romance
   Plays false with our affections;
Unsanctifies our tears – made sport
   For fanciful dejections:

Ah, no! the visions of the past
 Sustain the heart in feeling
Life as she is – our changeful Life,
 With friends and kindred dealing.

Bear witness, Ye, whose thoughts that day
 In Yarrow's groves were centred;
Who through the silent portal arch
 Of mouldering Newark entered;
And clomb the winding stair that once
 Too timidly was mounted
By the 'last Minstrel', (not the last!)
 Ere he his Tale recounted.

Flow on for ever, Yarrow Stream!
 Fulfil thy pensive duty,
Well pleased that future Bards should chant
 For simple hearts thy beauty;
To dream-light dear while yet unseen,
 Dear to the common sunshine,
And dearer still, as now I feel,
 To memory's shadowy moonshine!

Lines written in Early Spring

I heard a thousand blended notes,
While in a grove I sate reclined,
In that sweet mood when pleasant thoughts
Bring sad thoughts to the mind.

To her fair works did Nature link
The human soul that through me ran;
And much it grieved my heart to think
What man has made of man.

Through primrose tufts, in that green bower,
The periwinkle trailed its wreaths;
And 'tis my faith that every flower
Enjoys the air it breathes.

The birds around me hopped and played,
Their thoughts I cannot measure: —
But the least motion which they made,
It seemed a thrill of pleasure.

The budding twigs spread out their fan,
To catch the breezy air;
And I must think, do all I can,
That there was pleasure there.

If this belief from heaven be sent,
If such be Nature's holy plan,
Have I not reason to lament
What man has made of man?

Ode to Duty

Stern Daughter of the Voice of God!
O Duty! if that name thou love
Who art a light to guide, a rod
To check the erring, and reprove;
Thou, who art victory and law
When empty terrors overawe;
From vain temptations dost set free;
And calm'st the weary strife of frail humanity!

There are who ask not if thine eye
Be on them; who, in love and truth,
Where no misgiving is, rely
Upon the genial sense of youth:
Glad Hearts! without reproach or blot;
Who do thy work, and know it not:
Oh! if through confidence misplaced
They fail, thy saving arms, dread Power! around them cast.

Serene will be our days and bright,
And happy will our nature be,
When love is an unerring light,
And joy its own security.
And they a blissful course may hold
Even now, who, not unwisely bold,
Live in the spirit of this creed;
Yet seek thy firm support, according to their need.

I, loving freedom, and untried;
No sport of every random gust,
Yet being to myself a guide,
Too blindly have reposed my trust:
And oft, when in my heart was heard
Thy timely mandate, I deferred
The task, in smoother walks to stray;
But thee I now would serve more strictly, if I may.

Through no disturbance of my soul,
Or strong compunction in me wrought,
I supplicate for thy control;
But in the quietness of thought:
Me this unchartered freedom tires;
I feel the weight of chance-desires:
My hopes no more must change their name,
I long for a repose that ever is the same.

Yet not the less would I throughout
Still act according to the voice
Of my own wish; and feel past doubt
That my submissiveness was choice:
Not seeking in the school of pride
For 'precepts over dignified',
Denial and restraint I prize
No farther than they bred a second Will more wise.

Stern Lawgiver! yet thou dost wear
The Godhead's most benignant grace;
Nor know we anything so fair
As is the smile upon thy face:
Flowers laugh before thee on their beds
And fragrance in thy footing treads;
Thou dost preserve the stars from wrong;
And the most ancient heavens, through Thee, are fresh and strong.

To humbler functions, awful Power!
I call thee: I myself commend
Unto thy guidance from this hour;
Oh, let my weakness have an end!
Give unto me, made lowly wise,
The spirit of self-sacrifice;
The confidence of reason give;
And in the light of truth thy Bondman let me live!

Character of the Happy Warrior

Who is the happy Warrior? Who is he
That every man in arms should wish to be?
– It is the generous Spirit, who, when brought
Among the tasks of real life, hath wrought
Upon the plan that pleased his boyish thought:
Whose high endeavours are an inward light
That makes the path before him always bright:
Who, with a natural instinct to discern
What knowledge can perform, is diligent to learn;
Abides by this resolve, and stops not there,
But makes his moral being his prime care;
Who, doomed to go in company with Pain,
And Fear, and Bloodshed, miserable train!
Turns his necessity to glorious gain;
In face of these doth exercise a power
Which is our human nature's highest dower;
Controls them and subdues, transmutes, bereaves
Of their bad influence, and their good receives:
By objects, which might force the soul to abate
Her feeling, rendered more compassionate;
Is placable – because occasions rise
So often that demand such sacrifice;
More skilful in self-knowledge, even more pure,
As tempted more; more able to endure,
As more exposed to suffering and distress;
Thence, also, more alive to tenderness.
– 'Tis he whose law is reason; who depends
Upon that law as on the best of friends;
Whence, in a state where men are tempted still
To evil for a guard against worse ill,
And what in quality or act is best
Doth seldom on a right foundation rest,
He labours good on good to fix, and owes
To virtue every triumph that he knows:

– Who, if he rise to station of command,
Rises by open means; and there will stand
On honourable terms, or else retire,
And in himself possess his own desire;
Who comprehends his trust, and to the same
Keeps faithful with a singleness of aim;
And therefore does not stoop, nor lie in wait
For wealth, or honours, or for worldly state;
Whom they must follow; on whose head must fall,
Like showers of manna, if they come at all:
Whose powers shed round him in the common strife,
Or mild concerns of ordinary life,
A constant influence, a peculiar grace;
But who, if he be called upon to face
Some awful moment to which Heaven has joined
Great issues, good or bad for human kind,
Is happy as a Lover; and attired
With sudden brightness, like a Man inspired;
And, through the heat of conflict, keeps the law
In calmness made, and sees what he foresaw;
Or if an unexpected call succeed,
Come when it will, is equal to the need:
– He who, though thus endued as with a sense
And faculty for storm and turbulence,
Is yet a Soul whose master-bias leans
To homefelt pleasures and to gentle scenes;
Sweet images! which, wheresoe'er he be,
Are at his heart; and such fidelity
It is his darling passion to approve;
More brave for this, that he hath much to love: –
'Tis, finally, the Man, who, lifted high,
Conspicuous object in a Nation's eye,
Or left unthought-of in obscurity, –
Who, with a toward or untoward lot,
Prosperous or adverse, to his wish or not –
Plays, in the many games of life, that one
Where what he most doth value must be won:

Whom neither shape of danger can dismay,
Nor thought of tender happiness betray;
Who, not content that former worth stand fast,
Looks forward, persevering to the last,
From well to better, daily self-surpast:
Who, whether praise of him must walk the earth
For ever, and to noble deeds give birth,
Or he must fall, to sleep without his fame,
And leave a dead unprofitable name –
Finds comfort in himself and in his cause;
And, while the mortal mist is gathering, draws
His breath in confidence of Heaven's applause:
This is the happy Warrior; this is He
That every Man in arms should wish to be.

Ode

COMPOSED ON MAY MORNING

While from the purpling east departs
    The star that led the dawn,
Blithe Flora from her couch upstarts,
    For May is on the lawn.
A quickening hope, a freshening glee,
    Foreran the expected Power,
Whose first-drawn breath from bush and tree
    Shakes off that pearly shower.

All Nature welcomes Her whose sway
    Tempers the year's extremes;
Who scattereth lustres o'er noon-day,
    Like morning's dewy gleams;
While mellow warble, sprightly trill,
    The tremulous heart excite:
And hums the balmy air to still
    The balance of delight.

Time was, blest Power! when youths and maids
    At peep of dawn would rise,
And wander forth, in forest glades
    Thy birth to solemnize.
Though mute the song – to grace the rite
    Untouched the hawthorn bough,
Thy Spirit triumphs o'er the slight;
    Man changes, but not Thou!

Thy feathered Lieges bill and wings
    In love's disport employ;
Warmed by thy influence, creeping things
    Awake to silent joy:
Queen art thou still for each gay plant
    Where the slim wild deer roves;
And served in depths where fishes haunt
    Their own mysterious groves.

Cloud-piercing peak, and trackless heath,
    Instinctive homage pay;
Nor wants the dim-lit cave a wreath
    To honour thee, sweet May!
Where cities fanned by thy brisk airs
    Behold a smokeless sky,
Their puniest flower-pot-nursling dares
    To open a bright eye.

And if, on this thy natal morn,
    The pole, from which thy name
Hath not departed, stands forlorn
    Of song and dance and game;
Still from the village-green a vow
    Aspires to thee addrest,
Wherever peace is on the brow,
    Or love within the breast.

Yes! where Love nestles thou canst teach
   The soul to love the more;
Hearts also shall thy lessons reach
   That never loved before.
Stript is the haughty one of pride,
   The bashful freed from fear,
While rising, like the ocean-tide,
   In flows the joyous year.

Hush, feeble lyre! weak words refuse
   The service to prolong!
To yon exulting thrush the Muse
   Entrusts the imperfect song;
His voice shall chant, in accents clear,
   Throughout the live-long day,
Till the first silver star appear,
   The sovereignty of May.

Ode:
Intimations of Immortality from Recollections of Early Childhood

> The Child is father of the Man;
> And I could wish my days to be
> Bound each to each by natural piety.

I

There was a time when meadow, grove, and stream,
The earth, and every common sight,
    To me did seem
   Apparelled in celestial light,
The glory and the freshness of a dream.
It is not now as it hath been of yore; –
    Turn wheresoe'er I may,
    By night or day,
The things which I have seen I now can see no more.

II

The Rainbow comes and goes,
　　And lovely is the Rose,
　　The Moon doth with delight
Look round her when the heavens are bare,
　　Waters on a starry night
　　Are beautiful and fair;
　The sunshine is a glorious birth;
　But yet I know, where'er I go,
That there hath past away a glory from the earth.

III

Now, while the birds thus sing a joyous song,
　And while the young lambs bound
　　As to the tabor's sound,
To me alone there came a thought of grief:
A timely utterance gave that thought relief,
　　And I again am strong:
The cataracts blow their trumpets from the steep;
No more shall grief of mine the season wrong;
I hear the Echoes through the mountains throng,
The Winds come to me from the fields of sleep,
　　And all the earth is gay;
　　　Land and sea
　Give themselves up to jollity,
　　And with the heart of May
　Doth every Beast keep holiday; –
　　Thou Child of Joy,
Shout round me, let me hear thy shouts, thou happy Shepherd-boy!

IV

Ye blessed Creatures, I have heard the call
　Ye to each other make; I see
The heavens laugh with you in your jubilee;
　My heart is at your festival,
　　My head hath its coronal,
The fullness of your bliss, I feel – I feel it all.

Oh evil day! if I were sullen
While Earth herself is adorning,
        This sweet May-morning,
And the Children are culling
        On every side,
In a thousand valleys far and wide,
Fresh flowers; while the sun shines warm,
And the Babe leaps up on his Mother's arm: —
        I hear, I hear, with joy I hear!
        — But there's a Tree, of many, one,
A single Field which I have looked upon,
Both of them speak of something that is gone:
        The Pansy at my feet
        Doth the same tale repeat:
Whither is fled the visionary gleam?
Where is it now, the glory and the dream?

v

Our birth is but a sleep and a forgetting:
The Soul that rises with us, our life's Star,
        Hath had elsewhere its setting,
        And cometh from afar:
        Not in entire forgetfulness,
        And not in utter nakedness,
But trailing clouds of glory do we come
        From God, who is our home:
Heaven lies about us in our infancy!
Shades of the prison-house begin to close
        Upon the growing Boy,
But He beholds the light, and whence it flows,
        He sees it in his joy;
The Youth, who daily farther from the east
        Must travel, still is Nature's Priest,
        And by the vision splendid
        Is on his way attended;
At length the Man perceives it die away,
And fade into the light of common day.

VI

Earth fills her lap with pleasures of her own;
Yearnings she hath in her own natural kind,
And, even with something of a Mother's mind,
      And no unworthy aim,
    The homely Nurse doth all she can
To make her Foster-child, her Inmate Man,
    Forget the glories he hath known,
And that imperial palace whence he came.

VII

Behold the Child among his new-born blisses,
A six years' Darling of a pigmy size!
See, where 'mid work of his own hand he lies,
Fretted by sallies of his mother's kisses,
With light upon him from his father's eyes!
See, at his feet, some little plant or chart,
Some fragment from his dream of human life,
Shaped by himself with newly-learned art;
     A wedding or a festival,
     A mourning or a funeral;
      And this hath now his heart,
      And unto this he frames his song:
       Then will he fit his tongue
To dialogues of business, love, or strife;
      But it will not be long
      Ere this be thrown aside,
      And with new joy and pride
The little Actor cons another part;
Filling from time to time his 'humorous stage'
With all the Persons, down to palsied Age,
That Life brings with her in her equipage;
      As if his whole vocation
      Were endless imitation.

VIII

Thou, whose exterior semblance doth belie
　　　Thy Soul's immensity;
Thou best Philosopher, who yet dost keep
Thy heritage, thou Eye among the blind,
That, deaf and silent, read'st the eternal deep,
Haunted for ever by the eternal mind, –
　　　Mighty Prophet! Seer blest!
　　　On whom those truths do rest,
Which we are toiling all our lives to find,
In darkness lost, the darkness of the grave;
Thou, over whom thy Immortality
Broods like the Day, a Master o'er a Slave,
A Presence which is not to be put by;
　　　To whom the grave
Is but a lonely bed without the sense or sight
　　　Of day or the warm light,
A place of thought where we in waiting lie;
Thou little Child, yet glorious in the might
Of heaven-born freedom on thy being's height,
Why with such earnest pains dost thou provoke
The years to bring the inevitable yoke,
Thus blindly with thy blessedness at strife?
Full soon thy Soul shall have her earthly freight,
And custom lie upon thee with a weight,
Heavy as frost, and deep almost as life!

IX

　　　O joy! that in our embers
　　　Is something that doth live,
　　　That nature yet remembers
　　　What was so fugitive!
The thought of our past years in me doth breed
Perpetual benediction: not indeed
For that which is most worthy to be blest;
Delight and liberty, the simple creed

Of Childhood, whether busy or at rest,
With new-fledged hope still fluttering in his breast: –
     Not for these I raise
     The song of thanks and praise;
   But for those obstinate questionings
   Of sense and outward things,
   Fallings from us, vanishings;
   Blank misgivings of a Creature
Moving about in worlds not realised,
High instincts before which our mortal Nature
Did tremble like a guilty Thing surprised:
    But for those first affections,
    Those shadowy recollections,
   Which, be they what they may,
Are yet the fountain-light of all our day,
Are yet a master-light of all our seeing;
   Uphold us, cherish, and have power to make
Our noisy years seem moments in the being
Of the eternal Silence; truths that wake,
     To perish never:
Which neither listlessness, nor mad endeavour,
     Nor Man nor Boy,
Nor all that is at enmity with joy,
Can utterly abolish or destroy!
    Hence in a season of calm weather
    Though inland far we be,
Our Souls have sight of that immortal sea
    Which brought us hither,
    Can in a moment travel thither,
And see the Children sport upon the shore,
And hear the mighty waters rolling evermore.

         x

Then sing, ye Birds, sing, sing a joyous song!
    And let the young Lambs bound
    As to the tabor's sound!

We in thought will join your throng,
    Ye that pipe and ye that play,
    Ye that through your hearts to-day
    Feel the gladness of the May!
What though the radiance which was once so bright
Be now for ever taken from my sight,
    Though nothing can bring back the hour
Of splendour in the grass, of glory in the flower;
    We will grieve not, rather find
    Strength in what remains behind;
    In the primal sympathy
    Which having been must ever be;
    In the soothing thoughts that spring
    Out of human suffering;
    In the faith that looks through death,
In years that bring the philosophic mind.

XI

And O, ye Fountains, Meadows, Hills, and Groves,
Forebode not any severing of our loves!
Yet in my heart of hearts I feel your might;
I only have relinquished one delight
To live beneath your more habitual sway.
I love the Brooks which down their channels fret,
Even more than when I tripped lightly as they;
The innocent brightness of a new-born Day
    Is lovely yet;
The Clouds that gather round the setting sun
Do take a sober colouring from an eye
That hath kept watch o'er man's mortality;
Another race hath been, and other palms are won.
Thanks to the human heart by which we live,
Thanks to its tenderness, its joys, and fears,
To me the meanest flower that blows can give
Thoughts that do often lie too deep for tears.

Michael

If from the public way you turn your steps
Up the tumultuous brook of Greenhead Ghyll,
You will suppose that with an upright path
Your feet must struggle; in such bold ascent
The pastoral mountains front you, face to face.
But courage! for around that boisterous brook
The mountains have all opened out themselves,
And made a hidden valley of their own.
No habitation can be seen; but they
Who journey thither find themselves alone
With a few sheep, with rocks and stones, and kites
That overhead are sailing in the sky.
It is in truth an utter solitude;
Nor should I have made mention of this Dell
But for one object which you might pass by,
Might see and notice not. Beside the brook
Appears a straggling heap of unhewn stones!
And to that simple object appertains
A story – unenriched by strange events,
Yet not unfit, I deem, for the fireside,
Or for the summer shade. It was the first
Of those domestic tales that spake to me
Of shepherds, dwellers in the valleys, men
Whom I already loved; not verily
For their own sakes, but for the fields and hills
Where was their occupation and abode.
And thence this Tale, while I was yet a Boy
Careless of books, yet having felt the power
Of Nature, by the gentle agency
Of gentle objects, led me on to feel
For passions that were not my own, and think
(At random and imperfectly indeed)
On man, the heart of man, and human life.

Therefore, although it be a history
Homely and rude, I will relate the same
For the delight of a few natural hearts;
And, with yet fonder feeling, for the sake
Of youthful Poets, who among these hills
Will be my second self when I am gone.

   Upon the forest-side in Grasmere Vale
There dwelt a Shepherd, Michael was his name;
An old man, stout of heart, and strong of limb.
His bodily frame had been from youth to age
Of an unusual strength: his mind was keen,
Intense and frugal, apt for all affairs,
And in his shepherd's calling he was prompt
And watchful more than ordinary men.
Hence had he learned the meaning of all winds,
Of blasts of every tone; and, oftentimes,
When others heeded not, He heard the South
Make subterraneous music, like the noise
Of bagpipers on distant highland hills.
The Shepherd, at such warning, of his flock
Bethought him, and he to himself would say,
'The winds are now devising work for me!'
And, truly, at all times, the storm, that drives
The traveller to a shelter, summoned him
Up to the mountains: he had been alone
Amid the heart of many thousand mists
That came to him, and left him, on the heights.
And grossly that man errs, who should suppose
That the green valleys, and the streams and rocks,
Were things indifferent to the Shepherd's thoughts.
Fields, where with cheerful spirits he had breathed
The common air; hills, which with vigorous step
He had so often climbed; which had impressed
So many incidents upon his mind
Of hardship, skill or courage, joy or fear;
Which, like a book, preserved the memory
Of the dumb animals, whom he had saved,

Had fed and sheltered, linking to such acts
The certainty of honourable gain;
Those fields, those hills – what could they less? had laid
Strong hold on his affections, were to him
A pleasurable feeling of blind love,
The pleasure that there is in life itself.
   His days had not been passed in singleness.
His Helpmate was a comely matron, old –
Though younger than himself full twenty years.
She was a woman of a stirring life,
Whose heart was in her house: two wheels she had
Of antique form; this large, for spinning wool;
That small, for flax; and if one wheel had rest
It was because the other was at work.
The Pair had but one inmate in their house,
An only Child, who had been born to them
When Michael, telling o'er his years, began
To deem that he was old, – in shepherd's phrase,
With one foot in the grave. This only Son,
With two brave sheep-dogs tried in many a storm,
The one of an inestimable worth,
Made all their household. I may truly say,
That they were as a proverb in the vale
For endless industry. When day was gone,
And from their occupations out of doors
The Son and Father were come home, even then,
Their labour did not cease; unless when all
Turned to the cleanly supper-board, and there,
Each with his mess of pottage and skimmed milk,
Sat round the basket piled with oaten cakes,
And their plain home-made cheese. Yet when the meal
Was ended, Luke (for so the Son was named)
And his old Father both betook themselves
To such convenient work as might employ
Their hands by the fireside; perhaps to card
Wool for the Housewife's spindle, or repair
Some injury done to sickle, flail, or scythe,

Or other implement of house or field.
  Down from the ceiling, by the chimney's edge,
That in our ancient uncouth country style
With huge and black projection overbrowed
Large space beneath, as duly as the light
Of day grew dim the Housewife hung a lamp;
An aged utensil, which had performed
Service beyond all others of its kind.
Early at evening did it burn – and late,
Surviving comrade of uncounted hours,
Which, going by from year to year, had found,
And left, the couple neither gay perhaps
Nor cheerful, yet with objects and with hopes,
Living a life of eager industry.
And now, when Luke had reached his eighteenth year,
There by the light of this old lamp they sate,
Father and Son, while far into the night
The Housewife plied her own peculiar work,
Making the cottage through the silent hours
Murmur as with the sound of summer flies.
This light was famous in its neighbourhood,
And was a public symbol of the life
That thrifty Pair had lived. For, as it chanced,
Their cottage on a plot of rising ground
Stood single, with large prospect, north and south,
High into Easedale, up to Dunmail-Raise,
And westward to the village near the lake;
And from this constant light, so regular
And so far seen, the House itself, by all
Who dwelt within the limits of the vale,
Both old and young, was named the EVENING STAR.
  Thus living on through such a length of years,
The Shepherd, if he loved himself, must needs
Have loved his Helpmate; but to Michael's heart
This son of his old age was yet more dear –
Less from instinctive tenderness, the same
Fond spirit that blindly works in the blood of all –

Than that a child, more than all other gifts
That earth can offer to declining man,
Brings hope with it, and forward-looking thoughts,
And stirrings of inquietude, when they
By tendency of nature needs must fail.
Exceeding was the love he bare to him,
His heart and his heart's joy! For oftentimes
Old Michael, while he was a babe in arms,
Had done him female service, not alone
For pastime and delight, as is the use
Of fathers, but with patient mind enforced
To acts of tenderness; and he had rocked
His cradle, as with a woman's gentle hand.

   And, in a later time, ere yet the Boy
Had put on boy's attire, did Michael love,
Albeit of a stern unbending mind,
To have the Young-one in his sight, when he
Wrought in the field, or on his shepherd's stool
Sate with a fettered sheep before him stretched
Under the large old oak, that near his door
Stood single, and from matchless depth of shade,
Chosen for the Shearer's covert from the sun,
Thence in our rustic dialect was called
The CLIPPING TREE, a name which yet it bears.
There, while they two were sitting in the shade,
With others round them, earnest all and blithe,
Would Michael exercise his heart with looks
Of fond correction and reproof bestowed
Upon the Child, if he disturbed the sheep
By catching at their legs, or with his shouts
Scared them, while they lay still beneath the shears.

   And when by Heaven's good grace the boy grew up
A healthy Lad, and carried in his cheeks
Two steady roses that were five years old;
Then Michael from a winter coppice cut
With his own hand a sapling, which he hooped
With iron, making it throughout in all

Due requisites a perfect shepherd's staff,
And gave it to the Boy; wherewith equipt
He as a watchman oftentimes was placed
At gate or gap, to stem or turn the flock;
And, to his office prematurely called,
There stood the urchin, as you will divine,
Something between a hindrance and a help;
And for this cause not always, I believe,
Receiving from his Father hire of praise;
Though nought was left undone which staff, or voice,
Or looks, or threatening gestures, could perform.

But soon as Luke, full ten years old, could stand
Against the mountain blasts; and to the heights,
Not fearing toil, nor length of weary ways,
He with his Father daily went, and they
Were as companions, why should I relate
That objects which the shepherd loved before
Were dearer now? that from the Boy there came
Feelings and emanations – things which were
Light to the sun and music to the wind;
And that the old man's heart seemed born again?

Thus in his Father's sight the Boy grew up:
And now, when he had reached his eighteenth year,
He was his comfort and his daily hope.

While in this sort the simple household lived
From day to day, to Michael's ear there came
Distressful tidings. Long before the time
Of which I speak, the Shepherd had been bound
In surety for his brother's son, a man
Of an industrious life, and ample means;
But unforeseen misfortunes suddenly
Had prest upon him; and old Michael now
Was summoned to discharge the forfeiture,
A grievous penalty, but little less
Than half his substance. This unlooked-for claim,
At the first hearing, for a moment took
More hope out of his life than he supposed

That any old man ever could have lost.
As soon as he had armed himself with strength
To look his trouble in the face, it seemed
The shepherd's sole resource to sell at once
A portion of his patrimonial fields.
Such was his first resolve; he thought again,
And his heart failed him. 'Isabel,' said he,
'I have been toiling more than seventy years,
And in the open sunshine of God's love
Have we all lived: yet if these fields of ours
Should pass into a stranger's hand, I think
That I could not lie quiet in my grave.
Our lot is a hard lot; the sun himself
Has scarcely been more diligent than I;
And I have lived to be a fool at last
To my own family. An evil man
That was, and made an evil choice, if he
Were false to us; and if he were not false,
There are ten thousand to whom loss like this
Had been no sorrow. I forgive him; – but
'Twere better to be dumb than to talk thus.

   When I began, my purpose was to speak
Of remedies and of a cheerful hope.
Our Luke shall leave us, Isabel; the land
Shall not go from us, and it shall be free;
He shall possess it, free as is the wind
That passes over it. We have, thou knowest,
Another kinsman – he will be our friend
In this distress. He is a prosperous man,
Thriving in trade – and Luke to him shall go,
And with his kinsman's help and his own thrift
He quickly will repair this loss, and then
He may return to us. If here he stay,
What can be done? Where everyone is poor,
What can be gained?'
                              At this the old Man paused.
And Isabel sat silent, for her mind

Was busy, looking back into past times.
There's Richard Bateman, thought she to herself,
He was a parish-boy – at the church-door
They made a gathering for him, shillings, pence
And halfpennies, wherewith the neighbours bought
A basket, which they filled with pedlar's wares;
And, with this basket on his arm, the lad
Went up to London, found a master there,
Who, out of many, chose the trusty boy
To go and overlook his merchandise
Beyond the seas; where he grew wondrous rich,
And left estates and monies to the poor.
And, at his birth-place, built a chapel, floored
With marbles which he sent from foreign lands.
These thoughts, and many others of like sort,
Passed quickly through the mind of Isabel,
And her face brightened. The old Man was glad,
And thus resumed: – 'Well, Isabel! this scheme
These two days has been meat and drink to me.
Far more than we have lost is left us yet.
– We have enough – I wish indeed that I
Were younger; – but this hope is a good hope.
– Make ready Luke's best garments, of the best
Buy for him more, and let us send him forth
To-morrow, or the next day, or to-night:
– If he *could* go, the Boy should go to-night.'
    Here Michael ceased, and to the fields went forth
With a light heart. The Housewife for five days
Was restless morn and night, and all day long
Wrought on with her best fingers to prepare
Things needful for the journey of her son.
But Isabel was glad when Sunday came
To stop her in her work: for, when she lay
By Michael's side, she through the last two nights
Heard him, how he was troubled in his sleep:
And when they rose at morning she could see
That all his hopes were gone. That day at noon

She said to Luke, when they two by themselves
Were sitting at the door, 'Thou must not go:
We have no other Child but thee to lose,
None to remember – do not go away,
For if thou leave thy Father he will die.'
The Youth made answer with a jocund voice;
And Isabel, when she had told her fears,
Recovered heart. That evening her best fare
Did she bring forth, and all together sat
Like happy people round a Christmas fire.

With daylight Isabel resumed her work;
And all the ensuing week the house appeared
As cheerful as a grove in Spring; at length
The expected letter from their kinsman came,
With kind assurances that he would do
His utmost for the welfare of the Boy;
To which, requests were added, that forthwith
He might be sent to him. Ten times or more
The letter was read over; Isabel
Went forth to show it to the neighbours round;
Nor was there at that time on English ground
A prouder heart than Luke's. When Isabel
Had to her house returned, the old Man said,
'He shall depart to-morrow.' To this word
The Housewife answered, talking much of things
Which, if at such short notice he should go,
Would surely be forgotten. But at length
She gave consent, and Michael was at ease.

Near the tumultuous brook of Greenhead Ghyll,
In that deep valley, Michael had designed
To build a Sheepfold; and, before he heard
The tidings of his melancholy loss,
For this same purpose he had gathered up
A heap of stones, which by the streamlet's edge
Lay thrown together, ready for the work.
With Luke that evening thitherward he walked:
And soon as they had reached the place he stopped,

And thus the old Man spake to him: – 'My Son,
To-morrow thou wilt leave me: with full heart
I look upon thee, for thou art the same
That wert a promise to me ere thy birth,
And all thy life hast been my daily joy.
I will relate to thee some little part
Of our two histories; 'twill do thee good
When thou art from me, even if I should touch
On things thou canst not know of. – After thou
First cam'st into the world – as oft befalls
To new-born infants – thou didst sleep away
Two days, and blessings from thy Father's tongue
Then fell upon thee. Day by day passed on,
And still I loved thee with increasing love.
Never to living ear came sweeter sounds
Than when I heard thee by our own fireside
First uttering, without words, a natural tune;
While thou, a feeding babe, didst in thy joy
Sing at thy Mother's breast. Month followed month,
And in the open fields my life was passed
And on the mountains; else I think that thou
Hadst been brought up upon thy Father's knees.
But we were playmates, Luke: among these hills,
As well thou knowest, in us the old and young
Have played together, nor with me didst thou
Lack any pleasure which a boy can know.'
Luke had a manly heart; but at these words
He sobbed aloud. The old Man grasped his hand,
And said, 'Nay, do not take it so – I see
That these are things of which I need not speak.
– Even to the utmost I have been to thee
A kind and a good Father: and herein
I but repay a gift which I myself
Received at others' hands; for, though now old
Beyond the common life of man, I still
Remember them who loved me in my youth.
Both of them sleep together: here they lived,

As all their Forefathers had done; and when
At length their time was come, they were not loth
To give their bodies to the family mould.
I wish that thou shouldst live the life they lived:
But 'tis a long time to look back, my Son,
And see so little gain from threescore years.
These fields were burthened when they came to me;
Till I was forty years of age, not more
Than half of my inheritance was mine.
I toiled and toiled; God blessed me in my work.
And till these three weeks past the land was free.
– It looks as if it never could endure
Another Master. Heaven forgive me, Luke,
If I judge ill for thee, but it seems good
That thou shouldst go.'

                    At this the old Man paused;
Then pointing to the stones near which they stood,
Thus, after a short silence, he resumed:
'This was a work for us; and now, my Son,
It is a work for me. But, lay one stone –
Here, lay it for me, Luke, with thine own hands.
Nay, Boy, be of good hope; – we both may live
To see a better day. At eighty-four
I still am strong and hale; – do thou thy part;
I will do mine. – I will begin again
With many tasks that were resigned to thee:
Up to the heights, and in among the storms,
Will I without thee go again, and do
All works which I was wont to do alone,
Before I knew thy face. – Heaven bless thee, Boy!
Thy heart these two weeks has been beating fast
With many hopes; it should be so – yes – yes –
I knew that thou couldst never have a wish
To leave me, Luke: thou hast been bound to me
Only by links of love: when thou art gone,
What will be left to us! – But I forget
My purposes. Lay now the corner-stone,

As I requested; and hereafter, Luke,
When thou art gone away, should evil men
Be thy companions, think of me, my Son,
And of this moment; hither turn thy thoughts,
And God will strengthen thee: amid all fear
And all temptation, Luke, I pray that thou
May'st bear in mind the life thy Fathers lived,
Who, being innocent, did for that cause
Bestir them in good deeds. Now, fare thee well –
When thou return'st, thou in this place wilt see
A work which is not here: a covenant
'Twill be between us; but, whatever fate
Befall thee, I shall love thee to the last,
And bear thy memory with me to the grave.'
    The Shepherd ended here; and Luke stooped down,
And, as his Father had requested, laid
The first stone of the Sheepfold. At the sight
The old Man's grief broke from him; to his heart
He pressed his Son, he kissed him and wept;
And to the house together they returned.
– Hushed was that House in peace, or seeming peace,
Ere the night fell: – with morrow's dawn the Boy
Began his journey, and when he had reached
The public way, he put on a bold face;
And all the neighbours, as he passed their doors,
Came forth with wishes and with farewell prayers,
That followed him till he was out of sight.
    A good report did from their Kinsman come,
Of Luke and his well-doing: and the Boy
Wrote loving letters, full of wondrous news,
Which, as the Housewife phrased it, were throughout
'The prettiest letters that were ever seen.'
Both parents read them with rejoicing hearts.
So, many months passed on: and once again
The Shepherd went about his daily work
With confident and cheerful thoughts; and now
Sometimes when he could find a leisure hour

He to that valley took his way, and there
Wrought at the Sheepfold. Meantime Luke began
To slacken in his duty; and, at length,
He in the dissolute city gave himself
To evil courses: ignominy and shame
Fell on him, so that he was driven at last
To seek a hiding-place beyond the seas.

   There is a comfort in the strength of love;
'Twill make a thing endurable, which else
Would overset the brain, or break the heart:
I have conversed with more than one who well
Remember the old Man, and what he was
Years after he had heard this heavy news.
His bodily frame had been from youth to age
Of an unusual strength. Among the rocks
He went, and still looked up to sun and cloud,
And listened to the wind; and, as before,
Performed all kinds of labour for his sheep,
And for the land, his small inheritance.
And to that hollow dell from time to time
Did he repair, to build the Fold of which
His flock had need. 'Tis not forgotten yet
The pity which was then in every heart
For the old Man – and 'tis believed by all
That many and many a day he thither went
And never lifted up a single stone.

   There, by the Sheepfold, sometimes was he seen
Sitting alone, or with his faithful Dog,
Then old, beside him, lying at his feet.
The length of full seven years, from time to time,
He at the building of this Sheepfold wrought,
And left the work unfinished when he died.
Three years, or little more, did Isabel
Survive her Husband: at her death the estate
Was sold, and went into a stranger's hand.
The cottage which was named the EVENING STAR
Is gone – the ploughshare has been through the ground

On which it stood; great changes have been wrought
In all the neighbourhood: – yet the oak is left
That grew beside their door; and the remains
Of the unfinished Sheepfold may be seen
Beside the boisterous brook of Greenhead Ghyll.

To a Skylark

Ethereal minstrel! pilgrim of the sky!
Dost thou despise the earth where cares abound?
Or, while the wings aspire, are heart and eye
Both with thy nest upon the dewy ground?
Thy nest which thou canst drop into at will,
Those quivering wings composed, that music still!

Leave to the nightingale her shady wood;
A privacy of glorious light is thine;
Whence thou dost pour upon the world a flood
Of harmony, with instinct more divine;
Type of the wise who soar, but never roam;
True to the kindred points of Heaven and Home!

SELECTIONS FROM

The Prelude

OR, GROWTH OF A POET'S MIND[*]

(1) Childhood

Fair seed-time had my soul, and I grew up
Fostered alike by beauty and by fear:
Much favoured in my birthplace, and no less
In that beloved Vale to which erelong
We were transplanted – there were we let loose
For sports of wider range. Ere I had told
Ten birth-days, when among the mountain-slopes
Frost, and the breath of frosty wind, had snapped
The last autumnal crocus, 'twas my joy
With store of springes o'er my shoulder hung
To range the open heights where woodcocks run
Among the smooth green turf. Through half the night,
Scudding away from snare to snare, I plied
That anxious visitation; – moon and stars
Were shining o'er my head. I was alone,
And seemed to be a trouble to the peace
That dwelt among them. Sometimes it befell
In these night wanderings, that a strong desire
O'erpowered my better reason, and the bird
Which was the captive of another's toil
Became my prey; and when the deed was done
I heard among the solitary hills
Low breathings coming after me, and sounds
Of undistinguishable motion, steps
Almost as silent as the turf they trod.

[*] Before reading these passages from *The Prelude* the reader should consider
Wordsworth's explanation of them printed on pp. 124–5.

Nor less when spring had warmed the cultured Vale,
Moved we as plunderers where the mother-bird
Had in high places built her lodge; though mean
Our object and inglorious, yet the end
Was not ignoble. Oh! when I have hung
Above the raven's nest, by knots of grass
And half-inch fissures in the slippery rock
But ill sustained, and almost (so it seemed)
Suspended by the blast that blew amain,
Shouldering the naked crag, oh, at that time
While on the perilous ridge I hung alone,
With what strange utterance did the loud dry wind
Blow through my ear! the sky seemed not a sky
Of earth – and with what motion moved the clouds!

Dust as we are, the immortal spirit grows
Like harmony in music; there is a dark
Inscrutable workmanship that reconciles
Discordant elements, makes them cling together
In one society. How strange that all
The terrors, pains, and early miseries,
Regrets, vexations, lassitudes interfused
Within my mind, should e'er have borne a part,
And that a needful part, in making up
The calm existence that is mine when I
Am worthy of myself! Praise to the end!
Thanks to the means which Nature deigned to employ;
Whether her fearless visitings, or those
That came with soft alarm, like hurtless light
Opening the peaceful clouds; or she may use
Severer interventions, ministry
More palpable, as best might suit her aim.

One summer evening (led by her) I found
A little boat tied to a willow tree
Within a rocky cave, its usual home.
Straight I unloosed her chain, and stepping in

Pushed from the shore. It was an act of stealth
And troubled pleasure, nor without the voice
Of mountain-echoes did my boat move on;
Leaving behind her still, on either side,
Small circles glittering idly in the moon,
Until they melted all into one track
Of sparkling light. But now, like one who rows,
Proud of his skill, to reach a chosen point
With an unswerving line, I fixed my view
Upon the summit of a craggy ridge,
The horizon's utmost boundary; far above
Was nothing but the stars and the grey sky.
She was an elfin pinnace; lustily
I dipped my oars into the silent lake,
And, as I rose upon the stroke, my boat
Went heaving through the water like a swan;
When, from behind that craggy steep till then
The horizon's bound, a huge peak, black and huge,
As if with voluntary power instinct
Upreared its head. I struck and struck again,
And growing still in stature the grim shape
Towered up between me and the stars, and still,
For so it seemed, with purpose of its own
And measured motion like a living thing,
Strode after me. With trembling oars I turned,
And through the silent water stole my way
Back to the covert of the willow tree;
There in her mooring-place I left my bark, –
And through the meadows homeward went, in grave
And serious mood; but after I had seen
That spectacle, for many days, my brain
Worked with a dim and undetermined sense
Of unknown modes of being; o'er my thoughts
There hung a darkness, call it solitude
Or blank desertion. No familiar shapes
Remained, no pleasant images of trees,
Of sea or sky, no colours of green fields;

But huge and mighty forms, that do not live
Like living men, moved slowly through the mind
By day, and were a trouble to my dreams.

Wisdom and Spirit of the universe!
Thou Soul that art the eternity of thought,
That givest to forms and images a breath
And everlasting motion, not in vain
By day or star-light thus from my first dawn
Of childhood didst thou intertwine for me
The passions that build up our human soul;
Not with the mean and vulgar works of man,
But with high objects, with enduring things –
With life and nature – purifying thus
The elements of feeling and of thought,
And sanctifying, by such discipline,
Both pain and fear, until we recognise
A grandeur in the beatings of the heart.
Nor was this fellowship vouchsafed to me
With stinted kindness. In November days,
When vapours rolling down the valley made
A lonely scene more lonesome, among woods,
At noon and 'mid the calm of summer nights,
When, by the margin of the trembling lake,
Beneath the gloomy hills homeward I went
In solitude, such intercourse was mine;
Mine was it in the fields both day and night,
And by the waters, all the summer long.

And in the frosty season, when the sun
Was set, and visible for many a mile
The cottage windows blazed through twilight gloom,
I heeded not their summons: happy time
It was indeed for all of us – for me
It was a time of rapture! Clear and loud
The village clock tolled six, – I wheeled about,
Proud and exulting like an untired horse

That cares not for his home. All shod with steel,
We hissed along the polished ice in games
Confederate, imitative of the chase
And woodland pleasures, – the resounding horn,
The pack loud chiming, and the hunted hare.
So through the darkness and the cold we flew,
And not a voice was idle; with the din
Smitten, the precipices rang aloud;
The leafless trees and every icy crag
Tinkled like iron; while far distant hills
Into the tumult sent an alien sound
Of melancholy not unnoticed, while the stars
Eastward were sparkling clear, and in the west
The orange sky of evening died away.
Not seldom from the uproar I retired
Into a silent bay, or sportively
Glanced sideway, leaving the tumultuous throng,
To cut across the reflex of a star
That fled, and, flying still before me, gleamed
Upon the glassy plain; and oftentimes,
When we had given our bodies to the wind,
And all the shadowy banks on either side
Came sweeping through the darkness, spinning still
The rapid line of motion, then at once
Have I, reclining back upon my heels,
Stopped short; yet still the solitary cliffs
Wheeled by me – even as if the earth had rolled
With visible motion her diurnal round!
Behind me did they stretch in solemn train,
Feebler and feebler, and I stood and watched
Till all was tranquil as a dreamless sleep.

(2) *Residence at Cambridge*

Beside the pleasant Mill of Trompington
I laughed with Chaucer in the hawthorn shade;

Heard him, while birds were warbling, tell his tales
Of amorous passion. And that gentle Bard,
Chosen by the Muses for their Page of State –
Sweet Spenser, moving through his clouded heaven
With the moon's beauty and the moon's soft pace,
I called him Brother, Englishman, and Friend!
Yea, our blind Poet, who, in his later day,
Stood almost single; uttering odious truth –
Darkness before, and danger's voice behind,
Soul awful – if the earth has ever lodged
An awful soul – I seemed to see him here
Familiarly, and in his scholar's dress
Bounding before me, yet a stripling youth –
A boy, no better, with his rosy cheeks
Angelical, keen eye, courageous look,
And conscious step of purity and pride.
Among the band of my compeers was one
Whom chance had stationed in the very room
Honoured by Milton's name. O temperate Bard!
Be it confest that, for the first time, seated
Within thy innocent lodge and oratory,
One of a festive circle, I poured out
Libations, to thy memory drank, till pride
And gratitude grew dizzy in a brain
Never excited by the fumes of wine
Before that hour, or since. Then, forth I ran
From the assembly; through a length of streets,
Ran, ostrich-like, to reach our chapel door
In not a desperate or opprobrious time,
Albeit long after the importunate bell
Had stopped, with wearisome Cassandra voice
No longer haunting the dark winter night.
Call back, O Friend! a moment to thy mind
The place itself and fashion of the rites.
With careless ostentation shouldering up
My surplice, through the inferior throng I clove
Of the plain Burghers, who in audience stood

On the last skirts of their permitted ground,
Under the pealing organ. Empty thoughts!
I am ashamed of them: and that great Bard,
And thou, O Friend! who in thy ample mind
Hast placed me high above my best deserts,
Ye will forgive the weakness of that hour,
In some of its unworthy vanities,
Brother to many more.

    And when thereafter to my father's house
The holidays returned me, there to find
That golden store of books which I had left,
What joy was mine! How often in the course
Of those glad respites, though a soft west wind
Ruffled the waters to the angler's wish,
For a whole day together, have I lain
Down by thy side, O Derwent! murmuring stream,
On the hot stones, and in the glaring sun,
And there have read, devouring as I read,
Defrauding the day's glory, desperate!
Till with a sudden bound of smart reproach,
Such as an idler deals with in his shame,
I to the sport betook myself again.
    A gracious spirit o'er this earth presides,
And o'er the heart of man: invisibly
It comes, to works of unreproved delight,
And tendency benign, directing those
Who care not, know not, think not what they do.
The tales that charm away the wakeful night
In Araby, romances; legends penned
For solace by dim light of monkish lamps;
Fictions, for ladies of their love, devised
By youthful squires; adventures endless, spun
By the dismantled warrior in old age,
Out of the bowels of those very schemes
In which his youth did first extravagate;
These spread like day, and something in the shape

Of these will live till man shall be no more.
Dumb yearnings, hidden appetites, are ours,
And *they must* have their food. Our childhood sits,
Our simple childhood, sits upon a throne
That hath more power than all the elements.
I guess not what this tells of Being past,
Nor what it augurs of the life to come;
But so it is, and, in that dubious hour,
That twilight when we first begin to see
This dawning earth, to recognise, expect,
And, in the long probation that ensues,
The time of trial, ere we learn to live
In reconcilement with our stinted powers;
To endure this state of meagre vassalage,
Unwilling to forego, confess, submit,
Uneasy and unsettled, yoke-fellows
To custom, mettlesome, and not yet tamed
And humbled down; – oh! then we feel, we feel,
We know where we have friends. Ye dreamers, then,
Forgers of daring tales! we bless you then,
Impostors, drivellers, dotards, as the ape
Philosophy will call you: *then* we feel
With what, and how great might ye are in league,
Who make our wish, our power, our thought a deed,
An empire, a possession, – ye whom time
And seasons serve; all Faculties; – to whom
Earth crouches, the elements are potter's clay,
Space like a heaven filled up with northern lights,
Here, nowhere, there, and everywhere at once.

    The Poet's soul was with me at that time;
Sweet meditations, the still overflow
Of present happiness, while future years
Lacked not anticipations, tender dreams,
No few of which have since been realised;
And some remain, hopes for my future life.
Four years and thirty, told this very week,

Have I been now a sojourner on earth,
By sorrow not unsmitten; yet for me
Life's morning radiance hath not left the hills,
Her dew is on the flowers. Those were the days
Which also first emboldened me to trust
With firmness, hitherto but slightly touched
By such a daring thought, that I might leave
Some monument behind me which pure hearts
Should reverence. The instinctive humbleness,
Maintained even by the very name and thought
Of printed books and authorship, began
To melt away; and further, the dread awe
Of mighty names was softened down and seemed
Approachable, admitting fellowship
Of modest sympathy. Such aspect now,
Though not familiarly, my mind put on,
Content to observe, to achieve, and to enjoy.

(3) *Residence in London*

Yet was the theatre my dear delight;
The very gilding, lamps and painted scrolls,
And all the mean upholstery of the place,
Wanted not animation, when the tide
Of pleasure ebbed but to return as fast
With the ever-shifting figures of the scene,
Solemn or gay: whether some beauteous dame
Advanced in radiance through a deep recess
Of thick entangled forest, like the moon
Opening the clouds; or sovereign king, announced
With flourishing trumpet, came in full-blown state
Of the world's greatness, winding round with train
Of courtiers, banners, and a length of guards;
Or captive led in abject weeds, and jingling
His slender manacles; or romping girl
Bounced, leapt, and pawed the air; or mumbling sire,

A scare-crow pattern of old age dressed up
In all the tatters of infirmity
All loosely put together, hobbled in,
Stumping upon a cane with which he smites,
From time to time, the solid boards, and makes them
Prate somewhat loudly of the whereabout
Of one so overloaded with his years.
But what of this! the laugh, the grin, grimace,
The antics striving to outstrip each other,
Were all received, the least of them not lost,
With an unmeasured welcome. Through the night,
Between the show, and many-headed mass
Of the spectators, and each several nook
Filled with its fray or brawl, how eagerly
And with what flashes, as it were, the mind
Turned this way – that way! sportive and alert
And watchful, as a kitten when at play,
While winds are eddying round her, among straws
And rustling leaves. Enchanting age and sweet!
Romantic almost, looked at through a space,
How small, of intervening years! For then,
Though surely no mean progress had been made
In meditations holy and sublime,
Yet something of a girlish child-like gloss
Of novelty survived for scenes like these;
Enjoyment haply handed down from times
When at a country-playhouse, some rude barn
Tricked out for that proud use, if I perchance
Caught, on a summer evening through a chink
In the old wall, an unexpected glimpse
Of daylight, the bare thought of where I was
Gladdened me more than if I had been led
Into a dazzling cavern of romance,
Crowded with Genii busy among works
Not to be looked at by the common sun.

(4) *Retrospect.— Love of Nature leading to Love of Man*

What sounds are those, Helvellyn, that are heard
Up to thy summit, through the depth of air
Ascending, as if distance had the power
To make the sounds more audible? What crowd
Covers, or sprinkles o'er, yon village green?
Crowd seems it, solitary hill! to thee,
Though but a little family of men,
Shepherds and tillers of the ground – betimes
Assembled with their children and their wives,
And here and there a stranger interspersed.
They hold a rustic fair – a festival,
Such as, on this side now, and now on that,
Repeated through his tributary vales,
Helvellyn, in the silence of his rest,
Sees annually, if clouds towards either ocean
Blown from their favourite resting-place, or mists
Dissolved, have left him an unshrouded head.
Delightful day it is for all who dwell
In this secluded glen, and eagerly
They give it welcome. Long ere heat of noon,
From byre or field the kine were brought; the sheep
Are penned in cotes; the chaffering is begun.
The heifer lows, uneasy at the voice
Of a new master; bleat the flocks aloud.
Booths are there none; a stall or two is here;
A lame man or a blind, the one to beg,
The other to make music; hither, too,
From far, with basket, slung upon her arm,
Of hawker's wares – books, pictures, combs, and pins –
Some aged woman finds her way again,
Year after year, a punctual visitant!
There also stands a speech-maker by rote,
Pulling the strings of his boxed raree-show;
And in the lapse of many years may come

Prouder itinerant, mountebank, or he
Whose wonders in a covered wain lie hid.
But one there is, the loveliest of them all,
Some sweet lass of the valley, looking out
For gains, and who that sees her would not buy?
Fruits of her father's orchard are her wares,
And with the ruddy produce she walks round
Among the crowd, half pleased with, half ashamed
Of her new office, blushing restlessly.
The children now are rich, for the old to-day
Are generous as the young; and, if content
With looking on, some ancient wedded pair
Sit in the shade together, while they gaze,
'A cheerful smile unbends the wrinkled brow,*
The days departed start again to life,
And all the scenes of childhood reappear,
Faint, but more tranquil, like the changing sun
To him who slept at noon and wakes at eve.'
Thus gaiety and cheerfulness prevail ,
Spreading from young to old, from old to young,
And no one seems to want his share. — Immense
Is the recess, the circumambient world
Magnificent, by which they are embraced:
They move about upon the soft green turf:
How little they, they and their doings, seem,
And all that they can further or obstruct!
Through utter weakness pitiably dear,
As tender infants are: and yet how great!
For all things serve them; them the morning light
Loves, as it glistens on the silent rocks;
And them the silent rocks, which now from high
Look down upon them; the reposing clouds;
The wild brooks prattling from invisible haunts;
And old Helvellyn, conscious of the stir
Which animates this day their calm abode.

* The five lines within quotation marks are from 'The Malvern Hills'
by Joseph Cottle.

With deep devotion, Nature, did I feel,
In that enormous City's turbulent world
Of men and things, what benefit I owed
To thee, and those domains of rural peace,
Where to the sense of beauty first my heart
Was opened; tract more exquisitely fair
Than that famed paradise of ten thousand trees,
Or Gehol's matchless gardens, for delight
Of the Tartarian dynasty composed
(Beyond that mighty wall, not fabulous,
China's stupendous mound) by patient toil
Of myriads and boon nature's lavish help;
There, in a clime from widest empire chosen,
Fulfilling (could enchantment have done more?)
A sumptuous dream of flowery lawns, with domes
Of pleasure sprinkled over, shady dells
For eastern monasteries, sunny mounts
With temples crested, bridges, gondolas,
Rocks, dens, and groves of foliage taught to melt
Into each other their obsequious hues,
Vanished and vanishing in subtle chase,
Too fine to be pursued; or standing forth
In no discordant opposition, strong
And gorgeous as the colours side by side
Bedded among rich plumes of tropic birds;
And mountains over all, embracing all;
And all the landscape, endlessly enriched
With waters running, falling, or asleep.

But lovelier far than this, the paradise
Where I was reared; in Nature's primitive gifts
Favoured no less, and more to every sense
Delicious, seeing that the sun and sky,
The elements, and seasons as they change,
Do find a worthy fellow-labourer there –
Man free, man working for himself, with choice
Of time, and place, and object; by his wants,

His comforts, native occupations, cares,
Cheerfully led to individual ends
Or social, and still followed by a train
Unwooed, unthought-of even – simplicity
And beauty, and inevitable grace.

Yea, when a glimpse of those imperial bowers
Would to a child be transport over-great,
When but a half-hour's roam through such a place
Would leave behind a dance of images,
That shall break in upon his sleep for weeks;
Even then the common haunts of the green earth,
And ordinary interests of man,
Which they embosom, all without regard
As both may seem, are fastening on the heart
Insensibly, each with the other's help.
For me, when my affections first were led
From kindred, friends, and playmates, to partake
Love for the human creature's absolute self,
That noticeable kindliness of heart
Sprang out of fountains, there abounding most,
Where sovereign Nature dictated the tasks
And occupations which her beauty adorned,
And Shepherds were the men that pleased me first;
Not such as Saturn ruled 'mid Latian wilds,
With arts and laws so tempered, that their lives
Left, even to us toiling in this late day,
A bright tradition of the golden age;
Not such as, 'mid Arcadian fastnesses
Sequestered, handed down among themselves
Felicity, in Grecian song renowned;
Nor such as – when an adverse fate had driven,
From house and home, the courtly band whose fortunes
Entered, with Shakespeare's genius, the wild woods
Of Arden – amid sunshine or in shade
Culled the best fruits of Time's uncounted hours,
Ere Phoebe sighed for the false Ganymede;

Or there where Perdita and Florizel
Together danced, Queen of the feast, and King;
Nor such as Spenser fabled. True it is,
That I had heard (what he perhaps had seen)
Of maids at sunrise bringing in from far
Their May-bush, and along the street in flocks
Parading with a song of taunting rhymes,
Aimed at the laggards slumbering within doors;
Had also heard, from those who yet remembered,
Tales of the May-pole dance, and wreaths that decked
Porch, door-way, or kirk-pillar; and of youths,
Each with his maid, before the sun was up,
By annual custom, issuing forth in troops,
To drink the waters of some sainted well,
And hang it round with garlands. Love survives;
But, for such purpose, flowers no longer grow:
The times, too sage, perhaps too proud, have dropped
These lighter graces; and the rural ways
And manners which my childhood looked upon
Were the unluxuriant produce of a life
Intent on little but substantial needs,
Yet rich in beauty, beauty that was felt.
But images of danger and distress,
Man suffering among awful Powers and Forms;
Of this I heard, and saw enough to make
Imagination restless; nor was free
Myself from frequent perils; nor were tales
Wanting, – the tragedies of former times,
Hazards and strange escapes, of which the rocks
Immutable, and everflowing streams,
Where'er I roamed, were speaking monuments.

Smooth life had flock and shepherd in old time,
Long springs and tepid winters, on the banks
Of delicate Galesus; and no less
Those scattered along Adria's myrtle shores:
Smooth life had herdsman, and his snow-white herd

To triumphs and to sacrificial rites
Devoted, on the inviolable stream
Of rich Clitumnus; and the goat-herd lived
As calmly, underneath the pleasant brows
Of cool Lucretilis, where the pipe was heard
Of Pan, Invisible God, thrilling the rocks
With tutelary music, from all harm
The fold protecting. I myself, mature
In manhood then, have seen a pastoral tract
Like one of these, where Fancy might run wild,
Though under skies less generous, less serene:
There, for her own delight had Nature framed
A pleasure-ground, diffused a fair expanse
Of level pasture, islanded with groves
And banked with woody risings; but the Plain
Endless, here opening widely out, and there
Shut up in lesser lakes or beds of lawn
And intricate recesses, creek or bay
Sheltered within a shelter, where at large
The shepherd strays, a rolling hut his home.
Thither he comes with spring-time, there abides
All summer, and at sunrise ye may hear
His flageolet to liquid notes of love
Attuned, or sprightly fife resounding far.
Nook is there none, nor tract of that vast space
Where passage opens, but the same shall have
In turn its visitant, telling there his hours
In unlaborious pleasure, with no task
More toilsome than to carve a beechen bowl
For spring or fountain, which the traveller finds,
When through the region he pursues at will
His devious course. A glimpse of such sweet life
I saw when, from the melancholy walls
Of Goslar, once imperial, I renewed
My daily walk along that wide champaign,
That, reaching to her gates, spreads east and west,
And northwards, from beneath the mountainous verge

Of the Hercynian forest. Yet, hail to you
Moors, mountains, headlands, and ye hollow vales,
Ye long deep channels for the Atlantic's voice,
Powers of my native region! Ye that seize
The heart with firmer grasp! Your snows and streams
Ungovernable, and your terrifying winds,
That howl so dismally for him who treads
Companionless your awful solitudes!
There, 'tis the shepherd's task the winter long
To wait upon the storms: of their approach
Sagacious, into sheltering coves he drives
His flock, and thither from the homestead bears
A toilsome burden up the craggy ways,
And deals it out, their regular nourishment
Strewn on the frozen snow. And when the spring
Looks out, and all the pastures dance with lambs,
And when the flock, with warmer weather, climbs
Higher and higher, him his office leads
To watch their goings, whatsoever track
The wanderers choose. For this he quits his home
At day-spring, and no sooner doth the sun
Begin to strike him with a fire-like heat,
Than he lies down upon some shining rock,
And breakfasts with his dog. When they have stolen,
As is their wont, a pittance from strict time,
For rest not needed or exchange of love,
Then from his couch he starts; and now his feet
Crush out a livelier fragrance from the flowers
Of lowly thyme, by Nature's skill enwrought
In the wild turf: the lingering dews of morn
Smoke round him, as from hill to hill he hies,
His staff protending like a hunter's spear,
Or by its aid leaping from crag to crag,
And o'er the brawling beds of unbridged streams.
Philosophy, methinks, at Fancy's call,
Might deign to follow him through what he does
Or sees in his day's march; himself he feels,

In those vast regions where his service lies,
A freeman, wedded to his life of hope
And hazard, and hard labour interchanged
With that majestic indolence so dear
To native man. A rambling schoolboy, thus
I felt his presence in his own domain,
As of a lord and master, or a power,
Or genius, under Nature, under God,
Presiding; and severest solitude
Had more commanding looks when he was there.
When up the lonely brooks on rainy days
Angling I went, or trod the trackless hills
By mists bewildered, suddenly mine eyes
Have glanced upon him distant a few steps,
In size a giant, stalking through thick fog,
His sheep like Greenland bears; or, as he stepped
Beyond the boundary line of some hill-shadow,
His form hath flashed upon me, glorified
By the deep radiance of the setting sun:
Or him have I descried in distant sky,
A solitary object and sublime,
Above all height! like an aerial cross
Stationed alone upon a spiry rock
Of the Chartreuse, for worship. Thus was man
Ennobled outwardly before my sight,
And thus my heart was early introduced
To an unconscious love and reverence
Of human nature; hence the human form
To me became an index of delight,
Of grace and honour, power and worthiness.
Meanwhile this creature – spiritual almost
As those of books, but more exalted far;
Far more of an imaginative form
Than the gay Corin of the groves, who lives
For his own fancies, or to dance by the hour,
In coronal, with Phyllis in the midst –
Was, for the purposes of kind, a man

With the most common; husband, father; learned,
Could teach, admonish; suffered with the rest
From vice and folly, wretchedness and fear;
Of this I little saw, cared less for it,
But something must have felt.

                 Call ye these appearances –
Which I beheld of shepherds in my youth,
This sanctity of Nature given to man –
A shadow, a delusion, ye who pore
On the dead letter, miss the spirit of things;
Whose truth is not a motion or a shape
Instinct with vital functions, but a block
Or waxen image which yourselves have made,
And ye adore! But blessed be the God
Of Nature and of Man that this was so;
That men before my inexperienced eyes
Did first present themselves thus purified,
Removed, and to a distance that was fit:
And so we all of us in some degree
Are led to knowledge, wheresoever led,
And howsoever; were it otherwise,
And we found evil fast as we find good
In our first years, or think that it is found,
How could the innocent heart bear up and live!
But doubly fortunate my lot; not here
Alone, that something of a better life
Perhaps was round me than it is the privilege
Of most to move in, but that first I looked
At man through objects that were great or fair;
First communed with him by their help. And thus
Was founded a sure safeguard and defence
Against the weight of meanness, selfish cares,
Coarse manners, vulgar passions, that beat in
On all sides from the ordinary world
In which we traffic. Starting from this point
I had my face turned toward the truth, began
With an advantage furnished by that kind

Of prepossession, without which the soul
Receives no knowledge that can bring forth good,
No genuine insight ever comes to her.
From the restraint of over-watchful eyes
Preserved, I moved about, year after year,
Happy, and now most thankful that my walk
Was guarded from too early intercourse
With the deformities of crowded life,
And those ensuing laughters and contempts,
Self-pleasing, which, if we would wish to think
With a due reverence on earth's rightful lord,
Here placed to be the inheritor of heaven,
Will not permit us; but pursue the mind,
That to devotion willingly would rise,
Into the temple and the temple's heart.

(5) *Imagination and Taste, how Impaired and Restored*

From Nature doth emotion come, and moods
Of calmness equally are Nature's gift:
This is her glory; these two attributes
Are sister horns that constitute her strength.
Hence Genius, born to thrive by interchange
Of peace and excitation, finds in her
His best and purest friend; from her receives
That energy by which he seeks the truth,
From her that happy stillness of the mind
Which fits him to receive it when unsought.

Such benefit the humblest intellects
Partake of, each in their degree; 'tis mine
To speak, what I myself have known and felt;
Smooth task! for words find easy way, inspired
By gratitude, and confidence in truth.
Long time in search of knowledge did I range
The field of human life, in heart and mind

Benighted; but the dawn beginning now
To re-appear, 'twas proved that not in vain
I had been taught to reverence a Power
That is the visible quality and shape
And image of right reason; that matures
Her processes by steadfast laws; gives birth
To no impatient or fallacious hopes,
No heat of passion or excessive zeal,
No vain conceits; provokes to no quick turns
Of self-applauding intellect; but trains
To meekness, and exalts by humble faith;
Holds up before the mind intoxicate
With present objects, and the busy dance
Of things that pass away, a temperate show
Of objects that endure; and by this course
Disposes her, when over-fondly set
On throwing off incumbrances, to seek
In man, and in the frame of social life,
Whate'er there is desirable and good
Of kindred permanence, unchanged in form
And function, or, through strict vicissitude
Of life and death, revolving. Above all
Were re-established now those watchful thoughts
Which, seeing little worthy or sublime
In what the Historian's pen so much delights
To blazon – power and energy detached
From moral purpose – early tutored me
To look with feelings of fraternal love
Upon the unassuming things that hold
A silent station in this beauteous world.

(6) *Conclusion*

In one of those excursions (may they ne'er
Fade from remembrance!) through the Northern tracts
Of Cambria ranging with a youthful friend,

I left Bethgelert's huts at couching-time,
And westward took my way, to see the sun
Rise, from the top of Snowdon. To the door
Of a rude cottage at the mountain's base
We came, and roused the shepherd who attends
The adventurous stranger's steps, a trusty guide;
Then, cheered by short refreshment, sallied forth.

It was a close, warm, breezeless summer night,
Wan, dull, and glaring, with a dripping fog
Low-hung and thick that covered all the sky;
But, undiscouraged, we began to climb
The mountain-side. The mist soon girt us round,
And, after ordinary travellers' talk
With our conductor, pensively we sank
Each into commerce with his private thoughts:
Thus did we breast the ascent, and by myself
Was nothing either seen or heard that checked
Those musings or diverted, save that once
The shepherd's lurcher, who, among the crags,
Had to his joy unearthed a hedgehog, teased
His coiled-up prey with barkings turbulent.
This small adventure, for even such it seemed
In that wild place and at the dead of night,
Being over and forgotten, on we wound
In silence as before. With forehead bent
Earthward, as if in opposition set
Against an enemy, I panted up
With eager pace, and no less eager thoughts.
Thus might we wear a midnight hour away,
Ascending at loose distance each from each,
And I, as chanced, the foremost of the band;
When at my feet the ground appeared to brighten,
And with a step or two seemed brighter still;
Nor was time given to ask or learn the cause,
For instantly a light upon the turf
Fell like a flash, and lo! as I looked up,

The Moon hung naked in a firmament
Of azure without cloud, and at my feet
Rested a silent sea of hoary mist.
A hundred hills their dusky backs unheaved
All over this still ocean; and beyond,
Far, far beyond, the solid vapours stretched,
In headlands, tongues, and promontory shapes,
Into the main Atlantic, that appeared
To dwindle, and give up his majesty,
Usurped upon far as the sight could reach.
Not so the ethereal vault; encroachment none
Was there, nor loss; only the inferior stars
Had disappeared, or shed a fainter light
In the clear presence of the full-orbed Moon,
Who, from her sovereign elevation, gazed
Upon the billowy ocean, as it lay
All meek and silent, save that through a rift –
Not distant from the shore whereon we stood,
A fixed, abysmal, gloomy, breathing-place –
Mounted the roar of waters, torrents, streams
Innumerable, roaring with one voice!
Heard over earth and sea, and, in that hour,
For so it seemed, felt by the starry heavens.

When into air had partially dissolved
That vision, given to spirits of the night
And three chance human wanderers, in calm thought
Reflected, it appeared to me the type
Of a majestic intellect, its acts
And its possessions, what it has and craves,
What in itself it is, and would become.
There I beheld the emblem of a mind
That feeds upon infinity, that broods
Over the dark abyss, intent to hear
Its voices issuing forth to silent light
In one continuous stream; a mind sustained
By recognitions of transcendent power,

In sense conducting to ideal form,
In soul of more than mortal privilege.
One function, above all, of such a mind
Had Nature shadowed there, by putting forth,
'Mid circumstances awful and sublime,
That mutual domination which she loves
To exert upon the face of outward things,
So moulded, joined, abstracted, so endowed
With interchangeable supremacy,
That men, least sensitive, see, hear, perceive,
And cannot choose but feel. The power, which all
Acknowledge when thus moved, which Nature thus
To bodily sense exhibits, is the express
Resemblance of that glorious faculty
That higher minds bear with them as their own.
This is the very spirit in which they deal
With the whole compass of the universe:
They from their native selves can send abroad
Kindred mutations; for themselves create
A like existence; and whene'er it dawns
Created for them, catch it, or are caught
By its inevitable mastery,
Like angels stopped upon the wing by sound
Of harmony from Heaven's remotest spheres.
Them the enduring and the transient both
Serve to exalt; they build up greatest things
From least suggestions; ever on the watch,
Willing to work and to be wrought upon,
They need not extraordinary calls
To rouse them; in a world of life they live,
By sensible impressions not enthralled,
But by their quickening impulse made more prompt
To hold fit converse with the spiritual world,
And with the generations of mankind
Spread over time, past, present, and to come,
Age after age, till Time shall be no more.
Such minds are truly from the Deity,

For they are Powers; and hence the highest bliss
That flesh can know is theirs – the consciousness
Of Whom they are, habitually infused
Through every image and through every thought,
And all affections by communion raised
From earth to heaven, from heaven to divine;
Hence endless occupation for the Soul,
Whether discursive or intuitive;
Hence cheerfulness for acts of daily life,
Emotions which best foresight need not fear,
Most worthy then of trust when most intense.
Hence, amid ills that vex and wrongs that crush
Our hearts – if here the words of Holy Writ
May with fit reverence be applied – that peace
Which passeth understanding, that repose
In moral judgments which from this pure source
Must come, or will by man be sought in vain.

Oh! who is he that hath his whole life long
Preserved, enlarged, this freedom in himself?
For this alone is genuine liberty:
Where is the favoured being who hath held
That course unchecked, unerring, and untired,
In one perpetual progress smooth and bright? –
A humbler destiny have we retraced,
And told of lapse and hesitating choice,
And backward wanderings along thorny ways:
Yet – compassed round by mountain solitudes,
Within whose solemn temple I received
My earliest visitations, careless then
Of what was given me; and which now I range,
A meditative, oft a suffering, man –
Do I declare in accents which, from truth
Deriving cheerful confidence, shall blend
Their modulations with these vocal streams –
That, whatsoever falls my better mind,
Revolving with the accidents of life,

May have sustained, that, howsoe'er misled,
Never did I, in quest of right and wrong,
Tamper with conscience from a private aim;
Nor was in any public hope the dupe
Of selfish passions; nor did ever yield
Wilfully to mean cares or low pursuits,
But shrank with apprehensive jealousy
From every combination which might aid
The tendency, too potent in itself,
Of use and custom to bow down the soul
Under a growing weight of vulgar sense,
And substitute a universe of death
For that which moves with light and life informed,
Actual, divine, and true. To fear and love,
To love as prime and chief, for there fear ends,
Be this ascribed; to early intercourse
In presence of sublime or beautiful forms,
With the adverse principles of pain and joy –
Evil as one is rashly named by men
Who know not what they speak. By love subsists
All lasting grandeur, by pervading love;
That gone, we are as dust. – Behold the fields
In balmy spring-time full of rising flowers
And joyous creatures; see that pair, the lamb
And the lamb's mother, and their tender ways
Shall touch thee to the heart; thou callest this love,
And not inaptly so, for love it is,
Far as it carries thee. In some green bower
Rest, and be not alone, but have thou there
The One who is thy choice of all the world:
There linger, listening, gazing, with delight
Impassioned, but delight how pitiable!
Unless this love by a still higher love
Be hallowed, love that breathes not without awe;
Love that adores, but on the knees of prayer
By heaven inspired; that frees from chains the soul,
Lifted, in union with the purest, best,

Of earth-born passions, on the wings of praise,
Bearing a tribute to the Almighty's throne.

   This spiritual Love acts not nor can exist
Without Imagination, which, in truth,
Is but another name for absolute power
And clearest insight, amplitude of mind,
And Reason in her most exalted mood.
This faculty hath been the feeding source
Of our long labour: we have traced the stream
From the blind cavern whence is faintly heard
Its natal murmur; followed it to light
And open day; accompanied its course
Among the ways of Nature, for a time
Lost sight of it bewildered and engulphed;
Then given it greeting as it rose once more
In strength, reflecting from its placid breast
The works of man and face of human life;
And lastly, from its progress have we drawn
Faith in life endless, the sustaining thought
Of human being, Eternity, and God.

   Imagination having been our theme,
So also hath that intellectual Love,
For they are each in each, and cannot stand
Dividually. – Here must thou be, O Man!
Power to thyself; no Helper hast thou here;
Here keepest thou in singleness thy state:
No other can divide with thee this work:
No secondary hand can intervene
To fashion this ability; 'tis thine,
The prime and vital principle is thine
In the recesses of thy nature, far
From any reach of outward fellowship;
Else is not thine at all. But joy to him
Oh, joy to him who here hath sown, hath laid
Here, the foundation of his future years!
For all that friendship, all that love can do,

All that a darling countenance can look
Or dear voice utter, to complete the man,
Perfect him, made imperfect in himself,
All shall be his: and he whose soul hath risen
Up to the height of feeling intellect
Shall want no humbler tenderness; his heart
Be tender as a nursing mother's heart;
Of female softness shall his life be full,
Of humble cares and delicate desires,
Mild interests and gentlest sympathies.

    Child of my parents! Sister of my soul!
Thanks in sincerest verse have been elsewhere
Poured out for all the early tenderness
Which I from thee imbibed: and 'tis most true
That later seasons owed to thee no less;
For, spite of thy sweet influence and the touch
Of kindred hands that opened out the springs
Of genial thought in childhood, and in spite
Of all that unassisted I had marked
In life or nature of those charms minute
That win their way into the heart by stealth,
Still, to the very going-out of youth,
I too exclusively esteemed *that* love,
And sought *that* beauty, which, as Milton sings,
Hath terror in it. Thou didst soften down
This over-sternness; but for thee, dear Friend!
My soul, too reckless of mild grace, had stood
In her original self too confident,
Retained too long a countenance severe;
A rock with torrents roaring, with the clouds
Familiar, and a favourite of the stars:
But thou didst plant its crevices with flowers,
Hang it with shrubs that twinkle in the breeze,
And teach the little birds to build their nests
And warble in its chambers. At a time
When Nature, destined to remain so long

Foremost in my affections, had fallen back
Into a second place, pleased to become
A handmaid to a nobler than herself,
When every day brought with it some new sense
Of exquisite regard for common things,
And all the earth was budding with these gifts
Of more refined humanity, thy breath,
Dear Sister! was a kind of gentler spring
That went before my steps. Thereafter came
One whom with thee friendship had early paired;
She came, nor more a phantom to adorn
A moment, but an inmate of the heart,
And yet a spirit, there for me enshrined
To penetrate the lofty and the low;
Even as one essence of pervading light
Shines in the brightest of ten thousand stars,
And the meek worm that feeds her lonely lamp
Couched in the dewy grass.
                              With such a theme,
Coleridge! with this my argument, of thee
Shall I be silent? O capacious Soul!
Placed on this earth to love and understand,
And from thy presence shed the light of love,
Shall I be mute, ere thou be spoken of?
Thy kindred influence to my heart of hearts
Did also find its way. Thus fear relaxed
Her overweening grasp; thus thoughts and things
In the self-haunting spirit learned to take
More rational proportions; mystery,
The incumbent mystery of sense and soul,
Of life and death, time and eternity,
Admitted more habitually a mild
Interposition – a serene delight
In closelier gathering cares, such as become
A human creature, howsoe'er endowed,
Poet, or destined for a humbler name;
And so the deep enthusiastic joy,

The rapture of the hallelujah sent
From all that breathes and is, was chastened, stemmed
And balanced by pathetic truth, by trust
In hopeful reason, leaning on the stay
Of Providence; and in reverence for duty,
Here, if need be, struggling with storms, and there
Strewing in peace life's humblest ground with herbs,
At every season green, sweet at all hours.

    And now, O Friend! this history is brought
To its appointed close: the discipline
And consummation of a Poet's mind,
In everything that stood most prominent,
Have faithfully been pictured; we have reached
The time (our guiding object from the first)
When we may, not presumptuously, I hope,
Suppose my powers so far confirmed, and such
My knowledge, as to make me capable
Of building up a Work that shall endure.
Yet much hath been omitted, as need was;
Of books how much! and even of the other wealth
That is collected among woods and fields,
Far more: for Nature's secondary grace
Hath hitherto been barely touched upon,
The charm more superficial that attends
Her works, as they present to Fancy's choice
Apt illustrations of the moral world,
Caught at a glance, or traced with curious pains.

    Finally, and above all, O Friend! (I speak
With due regret) how much is overlooked
In human nature and her subtle ways,
As studied first in our own hearts, and then
In life among the passions of mankind,
Varying their composition and their hue,
Where'er we move, under the diverse shapes
That individual character presents

To an attentive eye. For progress meet,
Along this intricate and difficult path,
Whate'er was wanting, something had I gained,
As one of many schoolfellows compelled,
On hardy independence, to stand up
Amid conflicting interests, and the shock
Of various tempers; to endure and note
What was not understood, though known to be;
Among the mysteries of love and hate,
Honour and shame, looking to right and left,
Unchecked by innocence too delicate,
And moral notions too intolerant,
Sympathies too contracted. Hence, when called
To take a station among men, the step
Was easier, the transition more secure,
More profitable also; for the mind
Learns from the timely exercise to keep
In wholesome separation the two natures,
The one that feels, the other that observes . . .

Oh! yet a few short years of useful life,
And all will be complete, thy race be run,
Thy monument of glory will be raised;
Then, though (too weak to tread the ways of truth)
This age fall back to old idolatry,
Though men return to servitude as fast
As the tide ebbs, to ignominy and shame
By nations sink together, we shall still
Find solace – knowing what we have learnt to know,
Rich in true happiness if allowed to be
Faithful alike in forwarding a day
Of firmer trust, joint labourers in the work
(Should Providence such grace to us vouchsafe)
Of their deliverance, surely yet to come.
Prophets of Nature, we to them will speak
A lasting inspiration, sanctified
By reason, blessed by faith: what we have loved,

Others will love, and we will teach them how;
Instruct them how the mind of man becomes
A thousand times more beautiful than the earth
On which he dwells, above this frame of things
(Which, 'mid all revolution in the hopes
And fears of men, doth still remain unchanged)
In beauty exalted, as it is itself
Of quality and fabric more divine.

SELECTIONS FROM

The Excursion

PREFACE TO THE EDITION OF 1814

The Title-page announces that this is only a portion of a poem;
and the Reader must be here apprised that it belongs to the second
part of a long and laborious Work, which is to consist of three
parts. – The Author will candidly acknowledge that, if the first
of these had been completed, and in such a manner as to satisfy
his own mind, he should have preferred the natural order of
publication, and have given that to the world first; but, as the
second division of the Work was designed to refer more to passing
events, and to an existing state of things, than the others were
meant to do, more continuous exertion was naturally bestowed
upon it, and greater progress made here than in the rest of the
poem; and as this part does not depend upon the preceding, to a
degree which will materially injure its own peculiar interest, the
Author, complying with the earnest entreaties of some valued
Friends, presents the following pages to the Public.

It may be proper to state whence the poem, of which 'The
Excursion' is a part, derives its Title of 'The Recluse'. – Several
years ago, when the Author retired to his native mountains, with
the hope of being enabled to construct a literary Work that might
live, it was a reasonable thing that he should take a review of his
own mind, and examine how far Nature and Education had
qualified him for such employment. As subsidiary to this pre-
paration, he undertook to record, in verse, the origin and pro-
gress of his own powers, as far as he was acquainted with them.
That Work, addressed to a dear Friend, most distinguished for his
knowledge and genius, and to whom the Author's Intellect is
deeply indebted, has been long finished; and the result of the
investigation which gave rise to it was a determination to compose
a philosophical poem, containing views of Man, Nature, and

Society; and to be entitled, 'The Recluse', as having for its prin-
cipal subject the sensations and opinions of a poet living in retire-
ment. – The preparatory poem is biographical, and conducts the
history of the Author's mind to the point when he was emboldened
to hope that his faculties were sufficiently matured for entering
upon the arduous labour which he had proposed to himself; and
the two Works have the same kind of relation to each other, if he
may so express himself, as the ante-chapel has to the body of a
gothic church. Continuing this allusion, he may be permitted to
add, that his minor Pieces, which have been long before the Public,
when they shall be properly arranged, will be found by the atten-
tive Reader to have such connection with the main Work as may
give them claim to be likened to the little cells, oratories, and
sepulchral recesses, ordinarily included in those edifices.

The Author would not have deemed himself justified in say-
ing, upon this occasion, so much of performances either un-
finished, or unpublished; if he had not thought that the labour
bestowed by him upon what he had heretofore and now laid
before the Public, entitled him to candid attention for such a
statement as he thinks necessary to throw light upon his en-
deavours to please and, he would hope, to benefit his country-
men. – Nothing further need be added, than that the first and
third parts of 'The Recluse' will consist chiefly of meditations
in the Author's own person; and that in the intermediate part
('The Excursion') the intervention of characters speaking is em-
ployed, and something of a dramatic form adopted.

It is not the Author's intention formally to announce a system
it was more animating to him to proceed in a different course;
and if he shall succeed in conveying to the mind clear thoughts,
lively images, and strong feelings, the Reader will have no diffi-
culty in extracting the system for himself. And in the meantime
the following passage, taken from the conclusion of the first book
of 'The Recluse', may be acceptable as a kind of *Prospectus* of the
design and scope of the whole Poem.

On Man, on Nature and on Human Life,
Musing in solitude, I oft perceive
Fair trains of imagery before me rise,
Accompanied by feelings of delight
Pure, or with no unpleasing sadness mixed;
And I am conscious of affecting thoughts
And dear remembrances, whose presence soothes
Or elevates the Mind, intent to weigh
The good and evil of our mortal state.
– To these emotions, whencesoe'er they come,
Whether from breath of outward circumstance,
Or from the Soul – an impulse to herself –
I would give utterance in numerous verse.
Of Truth, of Grandeur, Beauty, Love, and Hope,
And melancholy Fear subdued by Faith;
Of blessed consolations in distress;
Of moral strength, and intellectual Power;
Of joy in widest commonalty spread;
Of the individual Mind that keeps her own
Inviolate retirement, subject there
To Conscience only, and the law supreme
Of that Intelligence which governs all –
I sing: – 'fit audience let me find though few!'

So prayed, more gaining than he asked, the Bard –
In holiest mood. Urania, I shall need
Thy guidance, or a greater Muse, if such
Descend to earth or dwell in highest heaven!
For I must tread on shadowy ground, must sink
Deep – and, aloft ascending, breathe in worlds
To which the heaven of heavens is but a veil.
All strength – all terror, single or in bands,
That ever was put forth in personal form –
Jehovah – with his thunder, and the choir
Of shouting Angels, and the empyreal thrones –

I pass them unalarmed. Not Chaos, not
The darkest pit of lowest Erebus,
Nor aught of blinder vacancy, scooped out
By help of dreams – can breed such fear and awe
As fall upon us often when we look
Into our Minds, into the Mind of Man –
My haunt, and the main region of my song.
– Beauty – a living Presence of the earth,
Surpassing the most fair ideal Forms
Which craft of delicate Spirits hath composed
From earth's materials – waits upon my steps;
Pitches her tents before me as I move,
An hourly neighbour. Paradise, and groves
Elysian, Fortunate Fields – like those of old
Sought in the Atlantic Main – why should they be
A history only of departed things,
Or a mere fiction of what never was?
For the discerning intellect of Man,
When wedded to this goodly universe
In love and holy passion, shall find these
A simple produce of the common day.
– I, long before the blissful hour arrives,
Would chant, in lonely peace, the spousal verse
Of this great consummation: – and, by words
Which speak of nothing more than what we are,
Would I arouse the sensual from their sleep
Of Death, and win the vacant and the vain
To noble raptures; while my voice proclaims
How exquisitely the individual Mind
(And the progressive powers perhaps no less
Of the whole species) to the external World
Is fitted: – and how exquisitely, too –
Theme this but little heard of among men –
The external World is fitted to the Mind;
And the creation (by no lower name
Can it be called) which they with blended might
Accomplish: – this is our high argument.

– Such grateful haunts foregoing, if I oft
Must turn elsewhere – to travel near the tribes
And fellowships of men, and see ill sights
Of madding passions mutually inflamed;
Must hear Humanity in fields and groves
Pipe solitary anguish; or must hang
Brooding above the fierce confederate storm
Of sorrow, barricadoed evermore
Within the walls of cities – may these sounds
Have their authentic comment; that even these
Hearing, I be not downcast or forlorn! –
Descend, prophetic Spirit! that inspir'st
The human Soul of universal earth,
Dreaming on things to come; and dost possess
A metropolitan temple in the hearts
Of mighty Poets: upon me bestow
A gift of genuine insight; that my Song
With star-like virtue in its place may shine,
Shedding benignant influence, and secure,
Itself, from all malevolent effect
Of those mutations that extend their sway
Throughout the nether sphere! – And if with this
I mix more lowly matter; with the thing
Contemplated, describe the Mind and Man
Contemplating; and who, and what he was –
The transitory Being that beheld
This Vision; when and where, and how he lived; –
Be not this labour useless. If such theme
May sort with highest objects, then – dread Power!
Whose gracious favour is the primal source
Of all illumination, – may my Life
Express the image of a better time,
More wise desires, and simpler manners; – nurse
My Heart in genuine freedom: – all pure thoughts
Be with me; – so shall thy unfailing love
Guide, and support, and cheer me to the end!

The Wanderer

ARGUMENT

A summer forenoon. – The Author reaches a ruined Cottage upon a Common, and there meets with a revered Friend, the Wanderer, of whose education and course of life he gives an account. – The Wanderer, while resting under the shade of the Trees that surround the Cottage, relates the History of its last Inhabitant.

'Twas summer, and the sun had mounted high:
Southward the landscape indistinctly glared
Through a pale steam; but all the northern downs,
In clearest air ascending, showed far off
A surface dappled o'er with shadows flung
From brooding clouds; shadows that lay in spots
Determined and unmoved, with steady beams
Of bright and pleasant sunshine interposed;
To him most pleasant who on soft cool moss
Extends his careless limbs along the front
Of some huge cave, whose rocky ceiling casts
A twilight of its own, an ample shade,
Where the wren warbles, while the dreaming man,
Half conscious of the soothing melody,
With side-long eye looks out upon the scene,
By power of that impending covert, thrown
To finer distance. Mine was at that hour
Far other lot, yet with good hope that soon
Under a shade as grateful I should find
Rest, and be welcomed there to livelier joy.
Across a bare wide Common I was toiling
With languid steps that by the slippery turf
Were baffled; nor could my weak arm disperse
The host of insects gathering round my face,
And ever with me as I paced along.

Upon that open moorland stood a grove,
The wished-for port to which my course was bound.
Thither I came, and there, amid the gloom
Spread by a brotherhood of lofty elms,
Appeared a roofless Hut; four naked walls
That stared upon each other! – I looked round,
And to my wish and to my hope espied
The Friend I sought; a Man of reverend age,
But stout and hale, for travel unimpaired.
There was he seen upon the cottage-bench,
Recumbent in the shade, as if asleep;
An iron-pointed staff lay at his side.

Him had I marked the day before – alone
And stationed in the public way, with face
Turned toward the sun then setting, while that staff
Afforded, to the figure of the man
Detained for contemplation or repose,
Graceful support; his countenance as he stood
Was hidden from my view, and he remained
Unrecognised; but, stricken by the sight,
With slackened footsteps I advanced, and soon
A glad congratulation we exchanged
At such unthought-of meeting. – For the night
We parted, nothing willingly; and now
He by appointment waited for me here,
Under the covert of these clustering elms.

We were tried Friends: amid a pleasant vale,
In the antique market-village where was passed
My school-time, an apartment he had owned,
To which at intervals the Wanderer drew,
And found a kind of home or harbour there.
He loved me; from a swarm of rosy boys
Singled out me, as he in sport would say,
For my grave looks, too thoughtful for my years.
As I grew up, it was my best delight

To be his chosen comrade. Many a time,
On holidays, we rambled through the woods:
We sate – we walked; he pleased me with report
Of things which he had seen; and often touched
Abstrusest matter, reasonings of the mind
Turned inward; or at my request would sing
Old songs, the product of his native hills;
A skilful distribution of sweet sounds,
Feeding the soul, and eagerly imbibed
As cool refreshing water, by the care
Of the industrious husbandman, diffused
Through a parched meadow-ground, in time of drought.
Still deeper welcome found his pure discourse:
How precious when in riper days I learned
To weigh with care his words, and to rejoice
In the plain presence of his dignity!

    Oh! many are the Poets that are sown
By Nature; men endowed with highest gifts,
The vision and the faculty divine:
Yet wanting the accomplishment of verse,
(Which, in the docile season of their youth,
It was denied them to acquire, through lack
Of culture and the inspiring aid of books,
Or haply by a temper too severe,
Or a nice backwardness afraid of shame)
Nor having e'er, as life advanced, been led
By circumstance to take unto the height
The measure of themselves, these favoured Beings,
All but a scattered few, live out their time,
Husbanding that which they possess within,
And go to the grave, unthought of. Strongest minds
Are often those of whom the noisy world
Hears least; else surely this Man had not left
His graces unrevealed and unproclaimed.
But, as the mind was filled with inward light,
So not without distinction had he lived,

Beloved and honoured – far as he was known.
And some small portion of his eloquent speech,
And something that may serve to set in view
The feeling pleasures of his loneliness,
His observations, and the thoughts his mind
Had dealt with – I will here record in verse;
Which, if with truth it correspond, and sink
Or rise as venerable Nature leads,
The high and tender Muses shall accept
With gracious smile, deliberately pleased,
And listening Time reward with sacred praise.

Among the hills of Athol he was born;
Where, on a small hereditary farm,
An unproductive slip of rugged ground,
His Parents, with their numerous offspring, dwelt;
A virtuous household, though exceeding poor!
Pure livers were they all, austere and grave,
And fearing God; the very children taught
Stern self-respect, a reverence for God's word,
And an habitual piety, maintained
With strictness scarcely known on English ground.

From his sixth year, the Boy of whom I speak,
In summer, tended cattle on the hills;
But, through the inclement and the perilous days
Of long-continuing winter, he repaired,
Equipped with satchel, to a school, that stood
Sole building on a mountain's dreary edge,
Remote from view of city spire, or sound
Of minster clock! From that bleak tenement
He, many an evening, to his distant home
In solitude returning, saw the hills
Grow larger in the darkness; all alone
Beheld the stars come out above his head,
And travelled through the wood, with no one near
To whom he might confess the things he saw.

So the foundations of his mind were laid.
In such communion, not from terror free,
While yet a child, and long before his time,
Had he perceived the presence and the power
Of greatness; and deep feelings had impressed
So vividly great objects that they lay
Upon his mind like substances, whose presence
Perplexed the bodily sense. He had received
A precious gift; for, as he grew in years,
With these impressions would he still compare
All his remembrances, thoughts, shapes, and forms;
And, being still unsatisfied with aught
Of dimmer character, he thence attained
An active power to fasten images
Upon his brain; and on their pictured lines
Intensely brooded, even till they acquired
The liveliness of dreams. Nor did he fail,
While yet a child, with a child's eagerness
Incessantly to turn his ear and eye
On all things which the moving seasons brought
To feed such appetite — nor this alone
Appeased his yearning: — in the after-day
Of boyhood, many an hour in caves forlorn,
And 'mid the hollow depths of naked crags
He sate, and even in their fixed lineaments,
Or from the power of a peculiar eye,
Or by creative feeling overborne,
Or by predominance of thought oppressed,
Even in their fixed and steady lineaments
He traced an ebbing and a flowing mind,
Expression ever varying!
                              Thus informed,
He had small need of books; for many a tale
Traditionally round the mountains hung,
And many a legend, peopling the dark woods,
Nourished Imagination in her growth,
And gave the Mind that apprehensive power

By which she is made quick to recognise
The moral properties and scope of things.
But eagerly he read, and read again,
Whate'er the minister's old shelf supplied;
The life and death of martyrs, who sustained,
With will inflexible, those fearful pangs
Triumphantly displayed in records left
Of persecution, and the Covenant – times
Whose echo rings through Scotland to this hour!
And there, by lucky hap, had been preserved
A straggling volume, torn and incomplete,
That left half-told the preternatural tale,
Romance of giants, chronicle of fiends,
Profuse in garniture of wooden cuts
Strange and uncouth; dire faces, figures dire,
Sharp-kneed, sharp-elbowed, and lean-ankled too,
With long and ghostly shanks – forms which once seen
Could never be forgotten!
                              In his heart,
Where Fear sate thus, a cherished visitant,
Was wanting yet the pure delight of love
By sound diffused, or by the breathing air,
Or by the silent looks of happy things,
Or flowing from the universal face
Of earth and sky. But he had felt the power
Of Nature, and already was prepared,
By his intense conceptions, to receive
Deeply the lesson deep of love which he,
Whom Nature, by whatever means, has taught
To feel intensely, cannot but receive.

    Such was the Boy – but for the growing Youth
What soul was his, when, from the naked top
Of some bold headland, he beheld the sun
Rise up, and bathe the world in light! He looked –
Ocean and earth, the solid frame of earth
And ocean's liquid mass, in gladness lay

Beneath him: — Far and wide the clouds were touched,
And in their silent faces could he read
Unutterable love. Sound needed none,
Nor any voice of joy; his spirit drank
The spectacle: sensation, soul, and form,
All melted into him; they swallowed up
His animal being; in them did he live,
And by them did he live; they were his life.
In such access of mind, in such high hour
Of visitation from the living God,
Thought was not; in enjoyment it expired.
No thanks he breathed, he proffered no request;
Rapt into still communion that transcends
The imperfect offices of prayer and praise,
His mind was a thanksgiving to the powers
That made him; it was blessedness and love!

A Herdsman on the lonely mountain-tops,
Such intercourse was his, and in this sort
Was his existence oftentimes *possessed*.
O then how beautiful, how bright, appeared
The written promise! Early had he learned
To reverence the volume that displays
The mystery, the life which cannot die;
But in the mountains did he *feel* his faith.
All things, responsive to the writing, there
Breathed immortality, revolving life,
And greatness still revolving; infinite:
There littleness was not; the least of things
Seemed infinite; and there his spirit shaped
Her prospects, nor did he believe, — he *saw*.
What wonder if his being thus became
Sublime and comprehensive! Low desires,
Low thoughts had there no place; yet was his heart
Lowly; for he was meek in gratitude,
Oft as he called those ecstasies to mind,
And whence they flowed; and from them he acquired

Wisdom, which works thro' patience; thence he learned
In oft-recurring hours of sober thought
To look on Nature with a humble heart,
Self-questioned where it did not understand,
And with a superstitious eye of love.

So passed the time; yet to the nearest town
He duly went with what small overplus
His earnings might supply, and brought away
The book that most had tempted his desires
While at the stall he read. Among the hills
He gazed upon that mighty orb of song,
The divine Milton. Lore of different kind,
The annual savings of a toilsome life,
His Schoolmaster supplied; books that explain
The purer elements of truth involved
In lines and numbers, and, by charm severe,
(Especially perceived where nature droops
And feeling is suppressed) preserve the mind
Busy in solitude and poverty.
These occupations oftentimes deceived
The listless hours, while in the hollow vale,
Hollow and green, he lay on the green turf
In pensive idleness. What could he do,
Thus daily thirsting, in that lonesome life,
With blind endeavours? Yet, still uppermost,
Nature was at his heart as if he felt,
Though yet he knew not how, a wasting power
In all things that from her sweet influence
Might tend to wean him. Therefore with her hues,
Her forms, and with the spirit of her forms,
He clothed the nakedness of austere truth.
While yet he lingered in the rudiments
Of science, and among her simplest laws,
His triangles – they were the stars of heaven,
The silent stars! Oft did he take delight
To measure the altitude of some tall crag

That is the eagle's birthplace, or some peak
Familiar with forgotten years, that shows
Inscribed upon its visionary sides
The history of many a winter storm,
Or obscure records of the path of fire.

    And thus before his eighteenth year was told,
Accumulated feelings pressed his heart
With still increasing weight; he was o'er-powered
By Nature; by the turbulence subdued
Of his own mind; by mystery and hope,
And the first virgin passion of a soul
Communing with the glorious universe.
Full often wished he that the winds might rage
When they were silent: far more fondly now
Than in his earlier season did he love
Tempestuous nights – the conflict and the sounds
That live in darkness. From his intellect
And from the stillness of abstracted thought
He asked repose; and, failing oft to win
The peace required, he scanned the laws of light
Amid the roar of torrents, where they send
From hollow clefts up to the clearer air
A cloud of mist, that smitten by the sun
Varies its rainbow hues. But vainly thus,
And vainly by all other means, he strove
To mitigate the fever of his heart.

    In dreams, in study, and in ardent thought,
Thus was he reared; much wanting to assist
The growth of intellect, yet gaining more,
And every moral feeling of his soul
Strengthened and braced, by breathing in content
The keen, the wholesome, air of poverty,
And drinking from the well of homely life.
– But, from past liberty, and tried restraints,

He now was summoned to select the course
Of humble industry that promised best
To yield him no unworthy maintenance.
Urged by his Mother, he essayed to teach
A village-school – but wandering thoughts were then
A misery to him; and the Youth resigned
A task he was unable to perform.

That stern yet kindly Spirit, who constrains
The Savoyard to quit his naked rocks,
The freeborn Swiss to leave his narrow vales,
(Spirit attached to regions mountainous
Like their own steadfast clouds) did now impel
His restless mind to look abroad with hope.
– An irksome drudgery seems it to plod on,
Through hot and dusty ways, or pelting storm,
A vagrant Merchant under a heavy load
Bent as he moves, and needing frequent rest;
Yet do such travellers find their own delight;
And their hard service, deemed debasing now,
Gained merited respect in simpler times;
When squire, and priest, and they who round them dwelt
In rustic sequestration – all dependent
Upon the PEDLAR's toil – supplied their wants,
Or pleased their fancies, with the wares he brought.
Not ignorant was the Youth that still no few
Of his adventurous countrymen were led
By perseverance in this track of life
To competence and ease: – to him it offered
Attractions manifold; – and this he chose.
– His Parents on the enterprise bestowed
Their farewell benediction, but with hearts
Foreboding evil. From his native hills
He wandered far; much did he see of men,
Their manners, their enjoyments, and pursuits,
Their passions and their feelings; chiefly those
Essential and eternal in the heart,

That, 'mid the simpler forms of rural life,
Exist more simple in their elements,
And speak a plainer language. In the woods,
A lone Enthusiast, and among the fields,
Itinerant in this labour, he had passed
The better portion of his time; and there
Spontaneously had his affections thriven
Amid the bounties of the year, the peace
And liberty of nature; there he kept
In solitude and solitary thought
His mind in a just equipoise of love.
Serene it was, unclouded by the cares
Of ordinary life; unvexed, unwarped
By partial bondage. In his steady course,
No piteous revolutions had he felt,
No wild varieties of joy and grief.
Unoccupied by sorrow of its own,
His heart lay open; and, by nature tuned
And constant disposition of his thoughts
To sympathy with man, he was alive
To all that was enjoyed where'er he went,
And all that was endured; for, in himself
Happy, and quiet in his cheerfulness,
He had no painful pressure from without
That made him turn aside from wretchedness
With coward fears. He could *afford* to suffer
With those whom he saw suffer. Hence it came
That in our best experience he was rich,
And in the wisdom of our daily life.
For hence, minutely, in his various rounds,
He had observed the progress and decay
Of many minds, of minds and bodies too;
The history of many families;
How they had prospered; how they were o'erthrown
By passion or mischance, or such misrule
Among the unthinking masters of the earth
As makes the nations groan.

                        This active course
He followed till provision for his wants
Had been obtained; – the Wanderer then resolved
To pass the remnant of his days, untasked
With needless services, from hardship free.
His calling laid aside, he lived at ease:
But still he loved to pace the public roads
And the wild paths; and, by the summer's warmth
Invited, often would he leave his home
And journey far, revisiting the scenes
That to his memory were most endeared.
– Vigorous in health, of hopeful spirits, undamped
By wordly-mindedness or anxious care;
Observant, studious, thoughtful, and refreshed
By knowledge gathered up from day to day;
Thus had he lived a long and innocent life.

    The Scottish Church, both on himself and those
With whom from childhood he grew up, had held
The strong hand of her purity; and still
Had watched him with an unrelenting eye.
This he remembered in his riper age
With gratitude, and reverential thoughts.
But by the native vigour of his mind,
By his habitual wanderings out of doors,
By loneliness, and goodness, and kind works,
Whate'er, in docile childhood or in youth,
He had imbibed of fear or darker thought
Was melted all away; so true was this,
That sometimes his religion seemed to me
Self-taught, as of a dreamer in the woods;
Who to the model of his own pure heart
Shaped his belief, as grace divine inspired,
And human reason dictated with awe.
– And surely never did there live on earth
A man of kindlier nature. The rough sports
And teasing ways of children vexed not him;

Indulgent listener was he to the tongue
Of garrulous age; nor did the sick man's tale,
To his fraternal sympathy addressed,
Obtain reluctant hearing.
                                    Plain his garb;
Such as might suit a rustic Sire, prepared
For Sabbath duties; yet he was a man
Whom no one could have passed without remark.
Active and nervous was his gait; his limbs
And his whole figure breathed intelligence.
Time had compressed the freshness of his cheek
Into a narrower circle of deep red,
But had not tamed his eye; that, under brows
Shaggy and grey, had meanings which it brought
From years of youth; which, like a Being made
Of many Beings, he had wondrous skill
To blend with knowledge of the years to come,
Human, or such as lie beyond the grave.

                          *

So was He framed; and such his course of life
Who now, with no appendage but a staff,
The prized memorial of relinquished toils,
Upon that cottage-bench reposed his limbs,
Screened from the sun. Supine the Wanderer lay,
His eyes as if in drowsiness half shut,
The shadows of the breezy elms above
Dappling his face. He had not heard the sound
Of my approaching steps, and in the shade
Unnoticed did I stand some minutes' space.
At length I hailed him, seeing that his hat
Was moist with water-drops, as if the brim
Had newly scooped a running stream. He rose,
And ere our lively greeting into peace
Had settled, ''Tis,' said I, 'a burning day:
My lips are parched with thirst, but you, it seems,

Have somewhere found relief.' He, at the word,
Pointing towards a sweet-briar, bade me climb
The fence where that aspiring shrub looked out
Upon the public way. It was a plot
Of garden ground run wild, its matted weeds
Marked with the steps of those, whom, as they passed,
The gooseberry trees that shot in long lank slips,
Or currants, hanging from their leafless stems,
In scanty strings, had tempted to o'erleap
The broken wall. I looked around, and there,
Where two tall hedge-rows of thick alder boughs
Joined in a cold damp nook, espied a well
Shrouded with willow-flowers and plum fern.
My thirst I slaked, and, from the cheerless spot
Withdrawing, straightway to the shade returned
Where sate the old Man on the cottage-bench;
And, while, beside him, with uncovered head,
I yet was standing, freely to respire,
And cool my temples in the fanning air,
Thus did he speak. 'I see around me here
Things which you cannot see: we die, my Friend,
Nor we alone, but that which each man loved
And prized in his peculiar nook of earth
Dies with him, or is changed; and very soon
Even of the good is no memorial left.
– The poets, in their elegies and songs
Lamenting the departed, call the groves,
They call upon the hills and streams to mourn,
And senseless rocks; nor idly; for they speak,
In these their invocations, with a voice
Obedient to the strong creative power
Of human passion. Sympathies there are
More tranquil, yet perhaps of kindred birth,
That steal upon the meditative mind,
And grow with thought. Beside yon spring I stood,
And eyed its waters till we seemed to feel
One sadness, they and I. For them a bond

Of brotherhood is broken: time has been
When, every day, the touch of human hand
Dislodged the natural sleep that binds them up
In mortal stillness; and they ministered
To human comfort. Stooping down to drink,
Upon the slimy foot-stone I espied
The useless fragment of a wooden bowl,
Green with the moss of years, and subject only
To the soft handling of the elements:
There let it lie – how foolish are such thoughts!
Forgive them; – never – never did my steps
Approach this door but she who dwelt within
A daughter's welcome gave me, and I loved her
As my own child. Oh, Sir! the good die first,
And they whose hearts are dry as summer dust
Burn to the socket. Many a passenger
Hath blessed poor Margaret for her gentle looks
When she upheld the cool refreshment drawn
From that forsaken spring; and no one came
But he was welcome; no one went away
But that it seemed she loved him. She is dead,
The light extinguished of her lonely hut,
The hut itself abandoned to decay,
And she forgotten in the quiet grave.

'I speak,' continued he, 'of One whose stock
Of virtues bloomed beneath this lowly roof.
She was a Woman of a steady mind,
Tender and deep in her excess of love;
Not speaking much, pleased rather with the joy
Of her own thoughts: by some especial care
Her temper had been framed, as if to make
A Being, who by adding love to peace
Might live on earth a life of happiness.
Her wedded Partner lacked not on his side
The humble worth that satisfied her heart:
Frugal, affectionate, sober, and withal

Keenly industrious. She with pride would tell
That he was often seated at his loom,
In summer, ere the mower was abroad
Among the dewy grass, – in early spring,
Ere the last star had vanished. – They who passed
At evening, from behind the garden fence
Might hear his busy spade, which he would ply,
After his daily work, until the light
Had failed, and every leaf and flower were lost
In the dark hedges. So their days were spent
In peace and comfort; and a pretty boy
Was their best hope, next to the God in heaven.

'Not twenty years ago, but you I think
Can scarcely bear it now in mind, there came
Two blighting seasons, when the fields were left
With half a harvest. It pleased Heaven to add
A worse affliction in the plague of war:
This happy Land was stricken to the heart!
A Wanderer then among the cottages,
I, with my freight of winter raiment, saw
The hardships of that season: many rich
Sank down, as in a dream, among the poor;
And of the poor did many cease to be,
And their place knew them not. Meanwhile, abridged
Of daily comforts, gladly reconciled
To numerous self-denials, Margaret
Went struggling on through those calamitous years
With cheerful hope, until the second autumn,
When her life's Helpmate on a sick-bed lay,
Smitten with perilous fever. In disease
He lingered long; and, when his strength returned,
He found the little he had stored, to meet
The hour of accident or crippling age,
Was all consumed. A second infant now
Was added to the troubles of a time
Laden, for them and all of their degree,

With care and sorrow: shoals of artisans
From ill-requited labour turned adrift
Sought daily bread from public charity,
They, and their wives and children – happier far
Could they have lived as do the little birds
That peck along the hedge-rows, or the kite
That makes her dwelling on the mountain rocks!

'A sad reverse it was for him who long
Had filled with plenty, and possessed in peace,
This lonely Cottage. At the door he stood,
And whistled many a snatch of merry tunes
That had no mirth in them; or with his knife
Carved uncouth figures on the heads of sticks –
Then, not less idly, sought, through every nook
In house or garden, any casual work
Of use or ornament; and with a strange,
Amusing, yet uneasy, novelty,
He mingled, where he might, the various tasks
Of summer, autumn, winter, and of spring.
But this endured not; his good humour soon
Became a weight in which no pleasure was:
And poverty brought on a petted mood
And a sore temper: day by day he drooped,
And he would leave his work – and to the town
Would turn without an errand his slack steps;
Or wander here and there among the fields.
One while he would speak lightly of his babes,
And with a cruel tongue: at other times
He tossed them with a false unnatural joy:
And 'twas a rueful thing to see the looks
Of the poor innocent children. "Every smile,"
Said Margaret to me, here beneath these trees,
"Made my heart bleed." '
                          At this the Wanderer paused;
And, looking up to those enormous elms,
He said, ''Tis now the hour of deepest noon.

At this still season of repose and peace,
This hour when all things which are not at rest
Are cheerful; while this multitude of flies
With tuneful hum is filling all the air;
Why should a tear be on an old Man's cheek?
Why should we thus, with an untoward mind,
And in the weakness of humanity,
From natural wisdom turn our hearts away;
To natural comfort shut our eyes and ears;
And, feeding on disquiet, thus disturb
The calm of nature with our restless thoughts?'

*

He spake with somewhat of a solemn tone:
But, when he ended, there was in his face
Such easy cheerfulness, a look so mild,
That for a little time it stole away
All recollection; and that simple tale
Passed from my mind like a forgotten sound.
A while on trivial things we held discourse,
To me soon tasteless. In my own despite,
I thought of that poor Woman as of one
Whom I had known and loved. He had rehearsed
Her homely tale with such familiar power,
With such an active countenance, an eye
So busy, that the things of which he spake
Seemed present; and, attention now relaxed,
A heart-felt chillness crept along my veins.
I rose; and, having left the breezy shade,
Stood drinking comfort from the warmer sun,
That had not cheered me long – ere, looking round
Upon that tranquil Ruin, I returned,
And begged of the old Man that, for my sake,
He would resume his story.

He replied,
'It were a wantonness, and would demand
Severe reproof, if we were men whose hearts
Could hold vain dalliance with the misery
Even of the dead; contented thence to draw
A momentary pleasure, never marked
By reason, barren of all future good.
But we have known that there is often found
In mournful thoughts, and always might be found,
A power to virtue friendly; were't not so,
I am a dreamer among men, indeed
An idle dreamer! 'Tis a common tale,
An ordinary sorrow of man's life,
A tale of silent suffering, hardly clothed
In bodily form. – But without further bidding
I will proceed.

    While thus it fared with them,
To whom this cottage, till those hapless years,
Had been a blessed home, it was my chance
To travel in a country far remote;
And when these lofty elms once more appeared
What pleasant expectations lured me on
O'er the flat Common! – With quick step I reached
The threshold, lifted with light hand the latch;
But, when I entered, Margaret looked at me
A little while; then turned her head away
Speechless, – and, sitting down upon a chair,
Wept bitterly. I wist not what to do,
Nor how to speak to her. Poor Wretch! at last
She rose from off her seat, and then, – O Sir!
I cannot *tell* how she pronounced my name: –
With fervent love, and with a face of grief
Unutterably helpless, and a look
That seemed to cling upon me, she enquired
If I had seen her husband. As she spake
A strange surprise and fear came to my heart,
Nor had I power to answer ere she told

That he had disappeared – not two months gone.
He left his house: two wretched days had past,
And on the third, as wistfully she raised
Her head from off her pillow, to look forth,
Like one in trouble, for returning light,
Within her chamber-casement she espied
A folded paper, lying as if placed
To meet her waking eyes. This tremblingly
She opened – found no writing, but beheld
Pieces of money carefully enclosed,
Silver and gold. "I shuddered at the sight,"
Said Margaret, "for I knew it was his hand
That must have placed it there; and ere that day
Was ended, that long anxious day, I learned,
From one who by my husband had been sent
With the sad news, that he had joined a troop
Of soldiers, going to a distant land.
– He left me thus – he could not gather heart
To take a farewell of me; for he feared
That I should follow with my babes, and sink
Beneath the misery of that wandering life."

    'This tale did Margaret tell with many tears:
And, when she ended, I had little power
To give her comfort, and was glad to take
Such words of hope from her own mouth as served
To cheer us both. But long we had not talked
Ere we built up a pile of better thoughts,
And with a brighter eye she looked around
As if she had been shedding tears of joy.
We parted. – 'Twas the time of early spring;
I left her busy with her garden tools;
And well remember, o'er that fence she looked,
And, while I paced along the foot-way path,
Called out, and sent a blessing after me,
With tender cheerfulness, and with a voice
That seemed the very sound of happy thoughts.

'I roved o'er many a hill and many a dale,
With my accustomed load; in heat and cold,
Through many a wood and many an open ground,
In sunshine and in shade, in wet and fair,
Drooping or blithe of heart, as might befall;
My best companions now the driving winds,
And now the "trotting brooks" and whispering trees,
And now the music of my own sad steps,
With many a short-lived thought that passed between,
And disappeared.
                 I journeyed back this way,
When, in the warmth of midsummer, the wheat
Was yellow; and the soft and bladed grass,
Springing afresh, had o'er the hay-field spread
Its tender verdure. At the door arrived,
I found that she was absent. In the shade,
Where now we sit, I waited her return.
Her cottage, then a cheerful object, wore
Its customary look, – only, it seemed,
The honeysuckle, crowding round the porch,
Hung down in heavier tufts; and that bright weed,
The yellow stone-crop, suffered to take root
Along the window's edge, profusely grew
Blinding the lower panes. I turned aside,
And strolled into her garden. It appeared
To lag behind the season, and had lost
Its pride of neatness. Daisy-flowers and thrift
Had broken their trim border-lines, and straggled
O'er paths they used to deck; carnations, once
Prized for surpassing beauty, and no less
For the peculiar pains they had required,
Declined their languid heads, wanting support.
The cumbrous bind-weed, with its wreaths and bells,
Had twined about her two small rows of peas,
And dragged them to the earth.
                      Ere this an hour
Was wasted. – Back I turned my restless steps;

A stranger passed; and, guessing whom I sought,
He said that she was used to ramble far. –
The sun was sinking in the west; and now
I sate with sad impatience. From within
Her solitary infant cried aloud;
Then, like a blast that dies away self-stilled,
The voice was silent. From the bench I rose;
But neither could divert nor soothe my thoughts.
The spot, though fair, was very desolate –
The longer I remained, more desolate:
And, looking round me, now I first observed
The corner stones, on either side the porch,
With dull red stains discoloured, and stuck o'er
With tufts and hairs of wool, as if the sheep
That fed upon the Common, thither came
Familiarly, and found a couching-place
Even at her threshold. Deeper shadows fell
From these tall elms; the cottage-clock struck eight; –
I turned, and saw her distant a few steps.
Her face was pale and thin – her figure, too,
Was changed. As she unlocked the door, she said,
"It grieves me you have waited here so long,
But, in good truth, I've wandered much of late;
And, sometimes – to my shame I speak – have need
Of my best prayers to bring me back again."
While on the board she spread our evening meal,
She told me – interrupting not the work
Which gave employment to her listless hands –
That she had parted with her elder child;
To a kind master on a distant farm
Now happily apprenticed. – "I perceive
You look at me, and you have cause; to-day
I have been travelling far; and many days
About the fields I wander, knowing this
Only, that what I seek I cannot find;
And so I waste my time: for I am changed;
And to myself," said she, "have done much wrong

And to this helpless infant. I have slept
Weeping, and weeping have I waked; my tears
Have flowed as if my body were not such
As others are; and I could never die.
But I am now in mind and in my heart
More easy; and I hope," said she, "that God
Will give me patience to endure the things
Which I behold at home."

         It would have grieved
Your very soul to see her. Sir, I feel
The story linger in my heart; I fear
'Tis long and tedious; but my spirit clings
To that poor Woman: – so familiarly
Do I perceive her manner, and her look,
And presence; and so deeply do I feel
Her goodness, that, not seldom, in my walks
A momentary trance comes over me;
And to myself I seem to muse on One
By sorrow laid asleep; or borne away,
A human being destined to awake
To human life, or something very near
To human life, when he shall come again
For whom she suffered. Yes, it would have grieved
Your very soul to see her: evermore
Her eyelids drooped, her eyes downward were cast;
And, when she at her table gave me food,
She did not look at me. Her voice was low,
Her body was subdued. In every act
Pertaining to her house-affairs, appeared
The careless stillness of a thinking mind
Self-occupied; to which all outward things
Are like an idle matter. Still she sighed,
But yet no motion of the breast was seen,
No heaving of the heart. While by the fire
We sate together, sighs came on my ear,
I knew not how, and hardly whence they came.

'Ere my departure, to her care I gave,
For her son's use, some tokens of regard,
Which with a look of welcome she received;
And I exhorted her to place her trust
In God's good love, and seek his help by prayer.
I took my staff, and, when I kissed her babe,
The tears stood in her eyes. I left her then
With the best hope and comfort I could give:
She thanked me for my wish; – but for my hope
It seemed she did not thank me.

                I returned,
And took my rounds along this road again
When on its sunny bank the primrose flower
Peeped forth, to give an earnest of the Spring.
I found her sad and drooping: she had learned
No tidings of her husband; if he lived,
She knew not that he lived; if he were dead,
She knew not he was dead. She seemed the same
In person and appearance; but her house
Bespake a sleepy hand of negligence;
The floor was neither dry nor neat, the hearth
Was comfortless, and her small lot of books,
Which, in the cottage-window, heretofore
Had been piled up against the corner panes
In seemly order, now, with straggling leaves
Lay scattered here and there, open or shut,
As they had chanced to fall. Her infant Babe
Had from its mother caught the trick of grief,
And sighed among its playthings. I withdrew,
And once again entering the garden saw,
More plainly still, that poverty and grief
Were now come nearer to her: weeds defaced
The hardened soil, and knots of withered grass:
No ridges there appeared of clear black mould,
No winter greenness; of her herbs and flowers,
It seemed the better part were gnawed away
Or trampled into earth; a chain of straw,

Which had been twined about the slender stem
Of a young apple-tree, lay at its root;
The bark was nibbled round by truant sheep.
– Margaret stood near, her infant in her arms,
And, noting that my eye was on the tree,
She said, "I fear it will be dead and gone
Ere Robert come again." When to the House
We had returned together, she enquired
If I had any hope: – but for her babe
And for her little orphan boy, she said,
She had no wish to live, that she must die
Of sorrow. Yet I saw the idle loom
Still in its place; his Sunday garments hung
Upon the self-same nail; his very staff
Stood undisturbed behind the door.
                                        And when,
In bleak December, I retraced this way,
She told me that her little babe was dead,
And she was left alone. She now, released
Form her maternal cares, had taken up
The employment common through these wilds, and gained,
By spinning hemp, a pittance for herself;
And for this end had hired a neighbour's boy
To give her needful help. That very time
Most willingly she put her work aside,
And walked with me along the miry road,
Heedless how far; and, in such piteous sort
That any heart had ached to hear her, begged
That, wheresoe'er I went, I still would ask
For him whom she had lost. We parted then –
Our final parting; for from that time forth
Did many seasons pass ere I returned
Into this tract again.
                          Nine tedious years;
From their first separation, nine long years,
She lingered in unquiet widowhood;
A Wife and Widow. Needs must it have been

A sore heart-wasting! I have heard, my Friend,
That in yon arbour oftentimes she sate
Alone, through half the vacant sabbath day;
And, if a dog passed by, she still would quit
The shade, and look abroad. On this old bench
For hours she sate; and evermore her eye
Was busy in the distance, shaping things
That made her heart beat quick. You see that path,
Now faint, – the grass has crept o'er its grey line;
There, to and fro, she paced through many a day
Of the warm summer, from a belt of hemp
That girt her waist, spinning the long-drawn thread
With backward steps. Yet ever as there passed
A man whose garment showed the soldier's red,
Or crippled mendicant in soldier's garb,
The little child who sate to turn the wheel
Ceased from his task; and she with faltering voice
Made many a fond enquiry; and when they,
Whose presence gave no comfort, were gone by,
Her heart was still more sad. And by yon gate,
That bars the traveller's road, she often stood,
And when a stranger horseman came, the latch
Would lift, and in his face look wistfully:
Most happy, if, from aught discovered there
Of tender feeling, she might dare repeat
The same sad question. Meanwhile her poor Hut
Sank to decay; for he was gone, whose hand,
At the first nipping of October frost,
Closed up each chink, and with fresh bands of straw
Chequered the green-grown thatch. And so she lived
Through the long winter, reckless and alone;
Until her house by frost, and thaw, and rain,
Was sapped; and while she slept, the nightly damps
Did chill her breast; and in the stormy day
Her tattered clothes were ruffled by the wind,
Even at the side of her own fire. Yet still
She loved this wretched spot, nor would for worlds

Have parted hence; and still that length of road,
And this rude bench, one torturing hope endeared,
Fast rooted at her heart: and here, my Friend, –
In sickness she remained; and here she died;
Last human tenant of these ruined walls!'

The old Man ceased: he saw that I was moved;
From that low bench, rising instinctively
I turned aside in weakness, nor had power
To thank him for the tale which he had told.
I stood, and leaning o'er the garden wall
Reviewed that Woman's sufferings; and it seemed
To comfort me while with a brother's love
I blessed her in the impotence of grief.
Then towards the cottage I returned; and traced
Fondly, though with an interest more mild,
That secret spirit of humanity
Which 'mid the calm oblivious tendencies
Of nature, 'mid her plants, and weeds, and flowers
And silent overgrowings, still survived.
The old Man, noting this, resumed, and said,
'My Friend! enough to sorrow you have given,
The purposes of wisdom ask no more:
Nor more would she have craved as due to One
Who, in her worst distress, had ofttimes felt
The unbounded might of prayer; and learned, with soul
Fixed on the Cross, that consolation springs,
From sources deeper far than deepest pain,
For the meek Sufferer. Why then should we read
The forms of things with an unworthy eye?
She sleeps in the calm earth, and peace is here.
I well remember that those very plumes,
Those weeds, and the high spear-grass on that wall,
By mist and silent rain-drops silvered o'er,
As once I passed, into my heart conveyed
So still an image of tranquillity,
So calm and still, and looked so beautiful

Amid the uneasy thoughts which filled my mind,
That what we feel of sorrow and despair
From ruin and from change, and all the grief
That passing shows of Being leave behind,
Appeared an idle dream, that could maintain,
Nowhere, dominion o'er the enlightened spirit
Whose meditative sympathies repose
Upon the breast of Faith. I turned away,
And walked along my road in happiness.'

He ceased. Ere long the sun declining shot
A slant and mellow radiance, which began
To fall upon us, while, beneath the trees,
We sate on that low bench: and now we felt,
Admonished thus, the sweet hour coming on.
A linnet warbled from those lofty elms,
A thrush sang loud, and other melodies,
At distance heard, peopled the milder air.
The old Man rose, and, with a sprightly mien
Of hopeful preparation, grasped his staff;
Together casting then a farewell look
Upon those silent walls, we left the shade;
And, ere the stars were visible, had reached
A village-inn, – our evening resting-place.

The Solitary

The Author describes his travels with the Wanderer, whose character is further
illustrated. – Morning scene, and view of a Village Wake. – Wanderer's account
of a Friend whom he purposes to visit. – View, from an eminence, of the Valley
which his Friend had chosen for his retreat. – Sound of singing from below. –
A funeral procession. – Descent into the Valley. – Observations drawn from
the Wanderer at sight of a book accidentally discovered in a recess in the
Valley. – Meeting with the Wanderer's friend, the Solitary. – Wanderer's
description of the mode of burial in this mountainous district. – Solitary con-
trasts with this, that of the individual carried a few minutes before from the

cottage. – The cottage entered. – Description of the Solitary's apartment. –
Repast there. – View, from the window, of two mountain summits; and the
Solitary's description of the companionship they afford him. – Account of the
departed inmate of the cottage. – Description of a grand spectacle upon the
mountains, with its effect upon the Solitary's mind. – Leave the house.

> In days of yore how fortunately fared
> The Minstrel! wandering on from hall to hall,
> Baronial court or royal; cheered with gifts
> Munificent, and love, and ladies' praise;
> Now meeting on his road an armed knight,
> Now resting with a pilgrim by the side
> Of a clear brook; – beneath an abbey's roof
> One evening sumptuously lodged; the next,
> Humbly in a religious hospital;
> Or with some merry outlaws of the wood;
> Or haply shrouded in a hermit's cell.
> Him, sleeping or awake, the robber spared;
> He walked – protected from the sword of war
> By virtue of that sacred instrument
> His harp, suspended at the traveller's side;
> His dear companion wheresoe'er he went
> Opening from land to land an easy way
> By melody, and by the charm of verse.
> Yet not the noblest of that honoured Race
> Drew happier, loftier, more empassioned, thoughts
> From his long journeyings and eventful life,
> Than this obscure Itinerant had skill
> To gather, ranging through the tamer ground
> Of these our unimaginative days;
> Both while he trod the earth in humblest guise
> Accoutred with his burthen and his staff;
> And now, when free to move with lighter pace.

> What wonder, then, if I, whose favourite school
> Hath been the fields, the roads, and rural lanes,
> Looked on this guide with reverential love?

Each with the other pleased, we now pursued
Our journey, under favourable skies.
Turn wheresoe'er we would, he was a light
Unfailing: not a hamlet could we pass,
Rarely a house, that did not yield to him
Remembrances; or from his tongue call forth
Some way-beguiling tale. Nor less regard
Accompanied those strains of apt discourse,
Which nature's various objects might inspire;
And in the silence of his face I read
His overflowing spirit. Birds and beasts,
And the mute fish that glances in the stream,
And harmless reptile coiling in the sun,
And gorgeous insect hovering in the air,
The fowl domestic, and the household dog –
In his capacious mind, he loved them all:
Their rights acknowledging he felt for all.
Oft was occasion given me to perceive
How the calm pleasures of the pasturing herd
To happy contemplation soothed his walk;
How the poor brute's condition, forced to run
Its course of suffering in the public road,
Sad contrast! all too often smote his heart
With unavailing pity. Rich in love
And sweet humanity, he was, himself,
To the degree that he desired, beloved.
Smiles of good-will from faces that he knew
Greeted us all day long; we took our seats
By many a cottage-hearth, where he received
The welcome of an Inmate from afar,
And I at once forgot I was a Stranger.
–Nor was he loth to enter ragged huts,
Huts where his charity was blest; his voice
Heard as the voice of an experienced friend.
And, sometimes – where the poor man held dispute
With his own mind, unable to subdue
Impatience through inaptness to perceive

General distress in his particular lot;
Or cherishing resentment, or in vain
Struggling against it; with a soul perplexed,
And finding in himself no steady power
To draw the line of comfort that divides
Calamity, the chastisement of Heaven,
From the injustice of our brother men –
To him appeal was made as to a judge;
Who, with an understanding heart, allayed
The perturbation; listened to the plea;
Resolved the dubious point; and sentence gave
So grounded, so applied, that it was heard
With softened spirit, even when it condemned.

Such intercourse I witnessed, while we roved,
Now as his choice directed, now as mine;
Or both, with equal readiness of will,
Our course submitting to the changeful breeze
Of accident. But when the rising sun
Had three times called us to renew our walk,
My Fellow-traveller, with earnest voice,
As if the thought were but a moment old,
Claimed absolute dominion for the day.
We started – and he led me toward the hills,
Up through an ample vale, with higher hills
Before us, mountains stern and desolate;
But, in the majesty of distance, now
Set off, and to our ken appearing fair
Of aspect, with aerial softness clad,
And beautified with morning's purple beams.

The wealthy, the luxurious, by the stress
Of business roused, or pleasure, ere their time,
May roll in chariots, or provoke the hoofs
Of the fleet coursers they bestride, to raise
From earth the dust of morning, slow to rise;

And they, if blest with health and hearts at ease,
Shall lack not their enjoyment: – but how faint
Compared with ours! who, pacing side by side,
Could, with an eye of leisure, look on all
That we beheld; and lend the listening sense
To every grateful sound of earth and air;
Pausing at will – our spirits braced, our thoughts
Pleasant as roses in the thickets blown,
And pure as dew bathing their crimson leaves.

Mount slowly, sun! that we may journey long,
By this dark hill protected from thy beams!
Such is the summer pilgrim's frequent wish;
But quickly from among our morning thoughts
'Twas chased away: for, toward the western side
Of the broad vale, casting a casual glance,
We saw a throng of people; – wherefore met?
Blithe notes of music, suddenly let loose
On the thrilled ear, and flags uprising, yield
Prompt answer; they proclaim the annual Wake,
Which the bright season favours. – Tabor and pipe
In purpose join to hasten or reprove
The laggard Rustic; and repay with boons
Of merriment a parti-coloured knot,
Already formed upon the village-green.
– Beyond the limits of the shadow cast
By the broad hill, glistened upon our sight
That gay assemblage. Round them and above,
Glitter, with dark recesses interposed,
Casement, and cottage-roof, and stems of trees
Half-veiled in vapoury cloud, the silver steam
Of dews fast melting on their leafy boughs
By the strong sunbeams smitten. Like a mast
Of gold, the Maypole shines; as if the rays
Of morning, aided by exhaling dew,
With gladsome influence could re-animate
The faded garlands dangling from its sides.

Said I, 'The music and the sprightly scene
Invite us; shall we quit our road, and join
These festive matins?' – He replied, 'Not loth
To linger I would here with you partake,
Not one hour merely, but till evening's close,
The simple pastimes of the day and place.
By the fleet Racers, ere the sun be set,
The turf of yon large pasture will be skimmed;
There, too, the lusty Wrestlers shall contend:
But know we not that he, who intermits
The appointed task and duties of the day,
Untunes full oft the pleasures of the day;
Checking the finer spirits that refuse
To flow, when purposes are lightly changed?
A length of journey yet remains untraced:
Let us proceed.' Then, pointing with his staff
Raised toward those craggy summits, his intent
He thus imparted: –

                    'In a spot that lies
Among yon mountain fastnesses concealed,
You will receive, before the hour of noon,
Good recompense, I hope, for this day's toil,
From sight of One who lives secluded there,
Lonesome and lost: of whom, and whose past life,
(Not to forestall such knowledge as may be
More faithfully collected from himself)
This brief communication shall suffice.

'Though now sojourning there, he, like myself,
Sprang from a stock of lowly parentage
Among the wilds of Scotland, in a tract
Where many a sheltered and well-tended plant
Bears, on the humblest ground of social life,
Blossoms of piety and innocence.
Such grateful promises his youth displayed:
And, having shown in study forward zeal,
He to the Ministry was duly called;

And straight, incited by a curious mind
Filled with vague hopes, he undertook the charge
Of Chaplain to a military troop
Cheered by the Highland bagpipe, as they marched
In plaided vest, – his fellow-countrymen.
This office filling, yet by native power
And force of native inclination made
An intellectual ruler in the haunts
Of social vanity, he walked the world,
Gay, and affecting graceful gaiety;
Lax, buoyant – less a pastor with his flock
Than a soldier among soldiers – lived and roamed
Where Fortune led: – and Fortune, who oft proves
The careless wanderer's friend, to him made known
A blooming Lady – a conspicuous flower,
Admired for beauty, for her sweetness praised;
Whom he had sensibility to love,
Ambition to attempt, and skill to win.

'For this fair Bride, most rich in gifts of mind,
Nor sparingly endowed with worldly wealth,
His office he relinquished; and retired
From the world's notice to a rural home –
Youth's season yet with him was scarcely past,
And she was in youth's prime. How free their love,
How full their joy! Till, pitiable doom!
In the short course of one undreaded year,
Death blasted all. Death suddenly o'erthrew
Two lovely Children – all that they possessed!
The Mother followed: – miserably bare
The one Survivor stood; he wept, he prayed
For his dismissal, day and night, compelled
To hold communion with the grave, and face
With pain the regions of eternity.
An uncomplaining apathy displaced
This anguish; and, indifferent to delight,
To aim and purpose, he consumed his days,

To private interest dead, and public care.
So lived he; so he might have died.
                                    But now,
To the wide world's astonishment, appeared
A glorious opening, the unlooked-for dawn,
That promised everlasting joy to France!
Her voice of social transport reached even him!
He broke from his contracted bounds, repaired
To the great City, an emporium then
Of golden expectations, and receiving
Freights every day from a new world of hope.
Thither his popular talents he transferred;
And, from the pulpit, zealously maintained
The cause of Christ and civil liberty,
As one, and moving to one glorious end.
Intoxicating service! I might say
A happy service; for he was sincere
As vanity and fondness for applause,
And new and shapeless wishes, would allow.

'That righteous cause (such power hath freedom) bound,
For one hostility, in friendly league,
Ethereal natures and the worst of slaves;
Was served by rival advocates that came
From regions opposite as heaven and hell.
One courage seemed to animate them all:
And, from the dazzling conquests daily gained
By their united efforts, there arose
A proud and most presumptuous confidence
In the transcendent wisdom of the age,
And her discernment; not alone in rights,
And in the origin and bounds of power
Social and temporal; but in laws divine,
Deduced by reason, or to faith revealed.
An overweening trust was raised; and fear
Cast out, alike of person and of thing.
Plague from this union spread, whose subtle bane

The strongest did not easily escape;
And He, what wonder! took a mortal taint.
How shall I trace the change, how bear to tell
That he broke faith with them whom he had laid
In earth's dark chambers, with a Christian's hope!
An infidel contempt of holy writ
Stole by degrees upon his mind; and hence
Life, like that Roman Janus, double-faced;
Vilest hypocrisy – the laughing, gay
Hypocrisy, not leagued with fear, but pride.
Smooth words he had to wheedle simple souls;
But, for disciples of the inner school,
Old freedom was old servitude, and they
The wisest whose opinions stooped the least
To known restraints; and who most boldly drew
Hopeful prognostications from a creed,
That, in the light of false philosophy,
Spread like a halo round a misty moon,
Widening its circle as the storms advance.

'His sacred function was at length renounced;
And every day and every place enjoyed
The unshackled layman's natural liberty;
Speech, manners, morals, all without disguise.
I do not wish to wrong him; though the course
Of private life licentiously displayed
Unhallowed actions – planted like a crown
Upon the insolent aspiring brow
Of spurious notions – worn as open signs
Of prejudice subdued – still he retained,
'Mid much abasement, what he had received
From nature, an intense and glowing mind.
Wherefore, when humbled Liberty grew weak,
And mortal sickness on her face appeared,
He coloured objects to his own desire
As with a lover's passion. Yet his moods
Of pain were keen as those of better men,

Nay keener, as his fortitude was less:
And he continued, when worse days were come,
To deal about his sparkling eloquence,
Struggling against the strange reverse with zeal
That showed like happiness. But, in despite
Of all this outside bravery, within,
He neither felt encouragement nor hope:
For moral dignity, and strength of mind,
Were wanting; and simplicity of life;
And reverence for himself; and, last and best,
Confiding thoughts, through love and fear of Him
Before whose sight the troubles of this world
Are vain, as billows in a tossing sea.

'The glory of the times fading away –
The splendour, which had given a festal air
To self-importance, hallowed it, and veiled
From his own sight – this gone, he forfeited
All joy in human nature; was consumed,
And vexed, and chafed, by levity and scorn,
And fruitless indignation; galled by pride;
Made desperate by contempt of men who throve
Before his sight in power or fame, and won,
Without desert, what he desired; weak men,
Too weak even for his envy or his hate!
Tormented thus, after a wandering course
Of discontent, and inwardly opprest
With malady – in part, I fear, provoked
By weariness of life – he fixed his home,
Or, rather say, sate down by very chance,
Among these rugged hills; where now he dwells,
And wastes the sad remainder of his hours,
Steeped in a self-indulging spleen, that wants not
Its own voluptuousness; – on this resolved,
With this content, that he will live and die
Forgotten, – at safe distance from "a world
Not moving to his mind." '

                                    These serious words
Closed the preparatory notices
That served my Fellow-traveller to beguile
The way, while we advanced up that wide vale.
Diverging now (as if his quest had been
Some secret of the mountains, cavern, fall
Of water, or some lofty eminence,
Renowned for splendid prospect far and wide)
We scaled, without a track to ease our steps,
A steep ascent; and reached a dreary plain,
With a tumultuous waste of huge hill tops
Before us; savage region! which I paced
Dispirited: when, all at once, behold!
Beneath our feet, a little lowly vale,
A lowly vale, and yet uplifted high
Among the mountains; even as if the spot
Had been from eldest time by wish of theirs
So placed, to be shut out from all the world!
Urn-like it was in shape, deep as an urn;
With rocks encompassed, save that to the south
Was one small opening, where a heath-clad ridge
Supplied a boundary less abrupt and close;
A quiet treeless nook, with two green fields,
A liquid pool that glittered in the sun,
And one bare dwelling; one abode, no more!
It seemed the home of poverty and toil,
Though not of want: the little fields, made green
By husbandry of many thrifty years,
Paid cheerful tribute to the moorland house.
– There crows the cock, single in his domain:
The small birds find in spring no thicket there
To shroud them; only from the neighbouring vales
The cuckoo, straggling up to the hill tops,
Shouteth faint tidings of some gladder place.

Ah! what a sweet Recess, thought I, is here!
Instantly throwing down my limbs at ease

Upon a bed of heath; – full many a spot
Of hidden beauty have I chanced to espy
Among the mountains; never one like this;
So lonesome, and so perfectly secure;
Not melancholy – no, for it is green,
And bright, and fertile, furnished in itself
With the few needful things that life requires.
– In rugged arms how softly does it lie,
How tenderly protected! Far and near
We have an image of the pristine earth,
The planet in its nakedness: were this
Man's only dwelling, sole appointed seat;
First, last, and single, in the breathing world,
It could not be more quiet: peace is here
Or nowhere; days unruffled by the gale
Of public news or private; years that pass
Forgetfully; uncalled upon to pay
The common penalties of mortal life,
Sickness, or accident, or grief, or pain.

On these and kindred thoughts intent I lay
In silence musing by my Comrade's side,
He also silent; when from out the heart
Of that profound abyss a solemn voice,
Or several voices in one solemn sound,
Was heard ascending; mournful, deep, and slow
The cadence, as of psalms – a funeral dirge!
We listened, looking down upon the hut,
But seeing no one: meanwhile from below
The strain continued, spiritual as before;
And now distinctly could I recognize
These words: – *'Shall in the grave thy love be known,
In death thy faithfulness?* – 'God rest his soul!'
Said the old man, abruptly breaking silence, –
'He is departed, and finds peace at last!'

This scarcely spoken, and those holy strains
Not ceasing, forth appeared in view a band

Of rustic persons, from behind the hut
Bearing a coffin in the midst, with which
They shaped their course along the sloping side
Of that small valley, singing as they moved;
A sober company and few, the men
Bare-headed, and all decently attired!
Some steps when they had thus advanced, the dirge
Ended; and, from the stillness that ensued
Recovering, to my Friend I said, 'You spake,
Methought, with apprehension that these rites
Are paid to Him upon whose shy retreat
This day we purposed to intrude.' – 'I did so,
But let us hence, that we may learn the truth:
Perhaps it is not he but some one else
For whom this pious service is performed;
Some other tenant of the solitude.'

   So, to a steep and difficult descent
Trusting ourselves, we wound from crag to crag,
Where passage could be won; and, as the last
Of the mute train, behind the heathy top
Of that off-sloping outlet, disappeared,
I, more impatient in my downward course,
Had landed upon easy ground; and there
Stood waiting for my Comrade. When behold
An object that enticed my steps aside!
A narrow, winding, entry opened out
Into a platform – that lay, sheepfold-wise,
Enclosed between an upright mass of rock
And one old moss-grown wall; – a cool recess,
And fanciful! For where the rock and wall
Met in an angle, hung a penthouse, framed
By thrusting two rude staves into the wall
And overlaying them with mountain sods;
To weather-fend a little turf-built seat
Whereon a full-grown man might rest, nor dread
The burning sunshine, or a transient shower;

But the whole plainly wrought by children's hands!
Whose skill had thronged the floor with a proud show
Of baby-houses, curiously arranged;
Nor wanting ornament of walks between,
With mimic trees inserted in the turf,
And gardens interposed. Pleased with the sight,
I could not choose but beckon to my Guide,
Who, entering, round him threw a careless glance
Impatient to pass on, when I exclaimed,
'Lo! what is here?' and, stooping down, drew forth
A book that, in the midst of stones and moss
And wreck of parti-coloured earthenware,
Aptly disposed, had lent its help to raise
One of those petty structures. 'His it must be!'
Exclaimed the Wanderer, 'cannot but be his,
And he is gone!' The book which in my hand
Had opened of itself (for it was swoln
With searching damp, and seemingly had lain
To the injurious elements exposed
From week to week,) I found to be a work
In the French tongue, a Novel of Voltaire,
His famous Optimist. 'Unhappy Man!'
Exclaimed my Friend: 'here then has been to him
Retreat within retreat, a sheltering place
Within how deep a shelter! He had fits,
Even to the last, of genuine tenderness,
And loved the haunts of children; here, no doubt
Pleasing and pleased, he shared their simple sports,
Or sate companionless; and here the book,
Left and forgotten in his careless way,
Must by the cottage-children have been found:
Heaven bless them, and their inconsiderate work!
To what odd purpose have the darlings turned
This sad memorial of their hapless friend!'

  'Me,' said I, 'most doth it surprise, to find
Such book in such a place!' – 'A book it is,'

He answered, 'to the Person suited well,
Though little suited to surrounding things:
'Tis strange, I grant; and stranger still had been
To see the Man who owned it, dwelling here,
With one poor shepherd, far from all the world! –
Now, if our errand hath been thrown away,
As from these intimations I forbode,
Grieved shall I be – less for my sake than yours,
And least of all for him who is no more.'

By this, the book was in the old Man's hand;
And he continued, glancing on the leaves
An eye of scorn: – 'The lover,' said he, 'doomed
To love when hope hath failed him – whom no depth
Of privacy is deep enough to hide,
Hath yet his bracelet or his lock of hair,
And that is joy to him. When change of times
Hath summoned kings to scaffolds, do but give
The faithful servant, who must hide his head
Henceforth in whatsoever nook he may,
A kerchief sprinkled with his master's blood,
And he too hath his comforter. How poor,
Beyond all poverty how destitute,
Must that Man have been left, who, hither driven,
Flying or seeking, could yet bring with him
No dearer relique, and no better stay,
Than this dull product of a scoffer's pen,
Impure conceits discharging from a heart
Hardened by impious pride! – I did not fear
To tax you with this journey;' mildly said
My venerable Friend, as forth we stepped
Into the presence of the cheerful light –
'For I have knowledge that you do not shrink
From moving spectacle; – but let us on.'

So speaking, on he went, and at the word
I followed, till he made a sudden stand:

For full in view, approaching through a gate
That opened from the enclosure of green fields
Into the rough uncultivated ground,
Behold the Man whom he had fancied dead!
I knew from his deportment, mien, and dress,
That it could be no other; a pale face,
A meagre person, tall, and in a garb
Not rustic – dull and faded like himself!
He saw us not, though distant but few steps;
For he was busy, dealing, from a store
Upon a broad leaf carried, choicest strings
Of red ripe currants; gift by which he strove,
With intermixture of endearing words,
To soothe a Child, who walked beside him, weeping
As if disconsolate. – 'They to the grave
Are bearing him, my Little-one,' he said,
'To the dark pit; but he will feel no pain;
His body is at rest, his soul in heaven.'

   More might have followed – but my honoured Friend
Broke in upon the Speaker with a frank
And cordial greeting. – Vivid was the light
That flashed and sparkled from the other's eyes;
He was all fire: no shadow on his brow
Remained, nor sign of sickness on his face.
Hands joined he with his Visitant, – a grasp,
An eager grasp; and many moments' space –
When the first glow of pleasure was no more,
And, of the sad appearance which at once
Had vanished, much was come and coming back –
An amicable smile retained the life
Which it had unexpectedly received,
Upon his hollow cheek. 'How kind,' he said,
'Nor could your coming have been better timed;
For this, you see, is in our narrow world
A day of sorrow. I have here a charge' –
And, speaking thus, he patted tenderly

The sun-burnt forehead of the weeping child –
'A little mourner, whom it is my task
To comfort; – but how came ye? – if yon track
(Which doth at once befriend us and betray)
Conducted hither your most welcome feet,
Ye could not miss the funeral train – they yet
Have scarcely disappeared.' 'This blooming Child,'
Said the old Man, 'is of an age to weep
At any grave or solemn spectacle,
Inly distressed or overpowered with awe,
He knows not wherefore; – but the boy to-day,
Perhaps is shedding orphan's tears; you also
Must have sustained a loss.' – 'The hand of Death,'
He answered, 'has been here; but could not well
Have fallen more lightly, if it had not fallen
Upon myself.' – The other left these words
Unnoticed, thus continuing. –
                                        'From yon crag
Down whose steep sides we dropped into the vale,
We heard the hymn they sang – a solemn sound
Heard anywhere; but in a place like this
'Tis more than human! Many precious rites
And customs of our rural ancestry
Are gone, or stealing from us; this, I hope,
Will last for ever. Oft on my way have I
Stood still, though but a casual passenger,
So much I felt the awfulness of life,
In that one moment when the corse is lifted
In silence, with a hush of decency;
Then from the threshold moves with song of peace,
And confidential yearnings, tow'rds its home,
Its final home on earth. What traveller – who –
(How far soe'er a stranger) does not own
The bond of brotherhood, when he sees them go,
A mute procession on the houseless road;
Or passing by some single tenement
Or clustered dwellings, where again they raise

The monitory voice? But most of all
It touches, it confirms, and elevates,
Then, when the body, soon to be consigned
Ashes to ashes, dust bequeathed to dust,
Is raised from the church-aisle, and forward borne
Upon the shoulders of the next in love,
The nearest in affection or in blood;
Yea, by the very mourners who had knelt
Beside the coffin, resting on its lid
In silent grief their unuplifted heads,
And heard meanwhile the Psalmist's mournful plaint,
And that most awful scripture which declares
We shall not sleep, but we shall all be changed!
– Have I not seen – ye likewise may have seen –
Son, husband, brothers – brothers side by side,
And son and father also side by side,
Rise from that posture: – and in concert move
On the green turf following the vested Priest,
Four dear supporters of one senseless weight,
From which they do not shrink, and under which
They faint not, but advance towards the open grave
Step after step – together, with their firm
Unhidden faces: he that suffers most,
He outwardly, and inwardly perhaps,
The most serene, with most undaunted eye! –
Oh! blest are they who live and die like these,
Loved with such love, and with such sorrow mourned!'

'That poor Man taken hence to-day,' replied
The Solitary, with a faint sarcastic smile
Which did not please me, 'must be deemed, I fear,
Of the unblest; for he will surely sink
Into his mother earth without such pomp
Of grief, depart without occasion given
By him for such array of fortitude.
Full seventy winters hath he lived, and mark!

This simple Child will mourn his one short hour,
And I shall miss him; scanty tribute! yet,
This wanting, he would leave the sight of men,
If love were his sole claim upon their care,
Like a ripe date which in the desert falls
Without a hand to gather it.'

                    At this
I interposed, though loth to speak, and said,
'Can it be thus among so small a band
As ye must needs be here? in such a place
I would not willingly, methinks, lose sight
Of a departing cloud.' – ''Twas not for love' –
Answered the sick Man with a careless voice –
'That I came hither; neither have I found
Among associates who have power of speech,
Nor in such other converse as is here,
Temptation so prevailing as to change
That mood, or undermine my first resolve.'
Then, speaking in like careless sort, he said
To my benign Companion, – 'Pity 'tis
That fortune did not guide you to this house
A few days earlier; then would you have seen
What stuff the Dwellers in a solitude,
That seems by Nature hollowed out to be
The seat and bosom of pure innocence,
Are made of; an ungracious matter this!
Which, for truth's sake, yet in remembrance too
Of past discussions with this zealous friend
And advocate of humble life, I now
Will force upon his notice; undeterred
By the example of his own pure course,
And that respect and deference which a soul
May fairly claim, by niggard age enriched
In what she most doth value, love of God
And his frail creature Man; – but ye shall hear.
I talk – and ye are standing in the sun
Without refreshment!'

                         Quickly had he spoken,
And, with light steps still quicker than his words,
Led toward the Cottage. Homely was the spot;
And, to my feeling, ere we reached the door,
Had almost a forbidding nakedness;
Less fair, I grant, even painfully less fair,
Than it appeared when from the beetling rock
We had looked down upon it. All within,
As left by the departed company,
Was silent; save the solitary clock
That on mine ear ticked with a mournful sound. –
Following our Guide, we clomb the cottage-stairs
And reached a small apartment dark and low,
Which was no sooner entered than our Host
Said gaily, 'This is my domain, my cell,
My hermitage, my cabin, what you will –
I love it better than a snail his house.
But now ye shall be feasted with our best.'

   So, with more ardour than an unripe girl
Left one day mistress of her mother's stores,
He went about his hospitable task.
My eyes were busy, and my thoughts no less,
And pleased I looked upon my grey-haired Friend,
As if to thank him; he returned that look,
Cheered, plainly, and yet serious. What a wreck
Had we about us! scattered was the floor,
And, in like sort, chair, window-seat, and shelf,
With books, maps, fossils, withered plants and flowers,
And tufts of mountain moss. Mechanic tools
Lay intermixed with scraps of paper, some
Scribbled with verse: a broken angling-rod
And shattered telescope, together linked
By cobwebs, stood within a dusty nook;
And instruments of music, some half-made,
Some in disgrace, hung dangling from the walls.
But speedily the promise was fulfilled

A feast before us, and a courteous Host
Inviting us in glee to sit and eat.
A napkin, white as foam of that rough brook
By which it had been bleached, o'erspread the board;
And was itself half-covered with a store
Of dainties, – oaten bread, curd, cheese, and cream;
And cakes of butter curiously embossed,
Butter that had imbibed from meadow-flowers
A golden hue, delicate as their own
Faintly reflected in a lingering stream.
Nor lacked, for more delight on that warm day,
Our table, small parade of garden fruits,
And whortle-berries from the mountain side.
The Child, who long ere this had stilled his sobs,
Was now a help to his late comforter,
And moved, a willing Page, as he was bid,
Ministering to our need.

                         In genial mood,
While at our pastoral banquet thus we sate
Fronting the window of that little cell,
I could not, ever and anon, forbear
To glance an upward look on two huge Peaks,
That from some other vale peered into this.
'Those lusty twins,' exclaimed our host, 'if here
It were your lot to dwell, would soon become
Your prized companions. – Many are the notes
Which, in his tuneful course, the wind draws forth
From rocks, woods, caverns, heaths, and dashing shores;
And well those lofty brethren bear their part
In the wild concert – chiefly when the storm
Rides high; then all the upper air they fill
With roaring sound, that ceases not to flow,
Like smoke, along the level of the blast,
In mighty current; theirs, too, is the song
Of stream and headlong flood that seldom fails;
And, in the grim and breathless hour of noon,
Methinks that I have heard them echo back

The thunder's greeting. Nor have nature's laws
Left them ungifted with a power to yield
Music of finer tone; a harmony,
So do I call it, though it be the hand
Of silence, though there be no voice; – the clouds,
The mist, the shadows, light of golden suns,
Motions of moonlight, all come thither – touch,
And have an answer – thither come, and shape
A language not unwelcome to sick hearts
And idle spirits: – there the sun himself,
At the calm close of summer's longest day,
Rests his substantial orb; – between those heights
And on the top of either pinnacle,
More keenly than elsewhere in night's blue vault,
Sparkle the stars, as of their station proud.
Thoughts are not busier in the mind of man
Than the mute agents stirring there: – alone
Here do I sit and watch. – '
                              A fall of voice,
Regretted like the nightingale's last note,
Had scarcely closed this high-wrought strain of rapture
Ere with inviting smile the Wanderer said:
'Now for the tale with which you threatened us!'
'In truth the threat escaped me unawares:
Should the tale tire you, let this challenge stand
For my excuse. Dissevered from mankind,
As to your eyes and thoughts we must have seemed
When ye looked down upon us from the crag,
Islanders 'mid a stormy mountain sea,
We are not so; – perpetually we touch
Upon the vulgar ordinances of the world;
And he, whom this our cottage hath to-day
Relinquished, lived dependent for his bread
Upon the laws of public charity.
The Housewife, tempted by such slender gains
As might from that occasion be distilled,
Opened, as she before had done for me,

Her doors to admit this homeless Pensioner;
The portion gave of coarse but wholesome fare
Which appetite required – a blind dull nook,
Such as she had, the *kennel* of his rest!
This, in itself not ill, would yet have been
Ill borne in earlier life; but his was now
The still contentedness of seventy years.
Calm did he sit under the wide-spread tree
Of his old age; and yet less calm and meek,
Winningly meek or venerably calm
Than slow and torpid; paying in this wise
A penalty, if penalty it were,
For spendthrift feats, excesses of his prime.
I loved the old Man, for I pitied him!
A task it was, I own, to hold discourse
With one so slow in gathering up his thoughts,
But he was a cheap pleasure to my eyes;
Mild, inoffensive, ready in *his* way,
And helpful to his utmost power: and there
Our housewife knew full well what she possessed!
He was her vassal of all labour, tilled
Her garden, from the pasture fetched her kine;
And, one among the orderly array
Of hay-makers, beneath the burning sun
Maintained his place; or heedfully pursued
His course, on errands bound, to other vales,
Leading sometimes an inexperienced child
Too young for any profitable task.
So moved he like a shadow that performed
Substantial service. Mark me now, and learn
For what reward! – The moon her monthly round
Hath not completed since our dame, the queen
Of this one cottage and this lonely dale,
Into my little sanctuary rushed –
Voice to a rueful treble humanized,
And features in deplorable dismay.
I treat the matter lightly, but, alas!

It is most serious: persevering rain
Had fallen in torrents; all the mountain-tops
Were hidden, and black vapours coursed their sides;
This had I seen, and saw; but, till she spake,
Was wholly ignorant that my ancient Friend –
Who at her bidding early and alone,
Had clomb aloft to delve the moorland turf
For winter fuel – to his noontide meal
Returned not, and now, haply, on the heights
Lay at the mercy of this raging storm.
"Inhuman" – said I, "was an old Man's life
Not worth the trouble of a thought? – alas!
This notice comes too late." With joy I saw
Her husband enter – from a distant vale.
We sallied forth together; found the tools
Which the neglected veteran had dropped,
But through all quarters looked for him in vain.
We shouted – but no answer! Darkness fell
Without remission of the blast or shower,
And fears for our own safety drove us home.

   'I, who weep little, did, I will confess,
The moment I was seated here alone,
Honour my little cell with some few tears
Which anger and resentment could not dry.
All night the storm endured; and, soon as help
Had been collected from the neighbouring vale,
With morning we renewed our quest: the wind
Was fallen, the rain abated, but the hills
Lay shrouded in impenetrable mist;
And long and hopelessly we sought in vain:
Till, chancing on that lofty ridge to pass
A heap of ruin – almost without walls
And wholly without roof (the bleached remains
Of a small chapel, where, in ancient time,
The peasants of these lonely valleys used
To meet for worship on that central height) –

We there espied the object of our search,
Lying full three parts buried among tufts
Of heath-plant, under and above him strewn,
To baffle, as he might, the watery storm:
And there we found him breathing peaceably,
Snug as a child that hides itself in sport
'Mid a green hay-cock in a sunny field.
We spake – he made reply, but would not stir
At our entreaty; less from want of power
Than apprehension and bewildering thoughts.

   'So was he lifted gently from the ground,
And with their freight homeward the shepherds moved
Through the dull mist, I following – when a step,
A single step, that freed me from the skirts
Of the blind vapour, opened to my view
Glory beyond all glory ever seen
By waking sense or by the dreaming soul!
The appearance, instantaneously disclosed,
Was of a mighty city – boldly say
A wilderness of building, sinking far
And self-withdrawn into a boundless depth,
Far sinking into splendour – without end!
Fabric it seemed of diamond and of gold,
With alabaster domes, and silver spires,
And blazing terrace upon terrace, high
Uplifted; here, serene pavilions bright,
In avenues disposed; there, towers begirt
With battlements that on their restless fronts
Bore stars – illumination of all gems!
By earthly nature had the effect been wrought
Upon the dark materials of the storm
Now pacified; on them, and on the coves
And mountain-steeps and summits, whereunto
The vapours had receded, taking there
Their station under a cerulean sky.
Oh, 'twas an unimaginable sight!

Clouds, mists, streams, watery rocks and emerald turf,
Clouds of all tincture, rocks and sapphire sky,
Confused, commingled, mutually inflamed,
Molten together, and composing thus,
Each lost in each, that marvellous array
Of temple, palace, citadel, and huge
Fantastic pomp of structure without name,
In fleecy folds voluminous, enwrapped.
Right in the midst, where interspace appeared
Of open court, an object like a throne
Under a shining canopy of state
Stood fixed; and fixed resemblances were seen
To implements of ordinary use,
But vast in size, in substance glorified;
Such as by Hebrew Prophets were beheld
In vision – forms uncouth of mightiest power
For admiration and mysterious awe.
This little Vale, a dwelling-place of Man,
Lay low beneath my feet; 'twas visible –
I saw not, but I felt that it was there.
That which I *saw* was the revealed abode
Of Spirits in beatitude: my heart
Swelled in my breast. – "I have been dead," I cried,
"And now I live! Oh! wherefore *do* I live?"
And with that pang I prayed to be no more! –
– But I forget our Charge, as utterly
I then forgot him: – there I stood and gazed:
The apparition faded not away,
And I descended.

       Having reached the house,
I found its rescued inmate safely lodged,
And in serene possession of himself,
Beside a fire whose genial warmth seemed met
By a faint shining from the heart, a gleam
Of comfort, spread over his pallid face.
Great show of joy the housewife made, and truly
Was glad to find her conscience set at ease;

And not less glad, for sake of her good name,
That the poor Sufferer had escaped with life.
But, though he seemed at first to have received
No harm, and uncomplaining as before
Went through his usual tasks, a silent change
Soon showed itself: he lingered three short weeks;
And from the cottage hath been borne to-day.

'So ends my dolorous tale, and glad I am
That it is ended.' At these words he turned –
And, with blithe air of open fellowship,
Brought from the cupboard wine and stouter cheer,
Like one who would be merry. Seeing this,
My grey-haired Friend said courteously – 'Nay, nay,
You have regaled us as a hermit ought;
Now let us forth into the sun!' – Our Host
Rose, though reluctantly, and forth we went.

Despondency Corrected

Editor's Note.

The next Book of 'The Excursion', omitted in this selection, is called
'Despondency' – a statement of the many experiences in the Solitary's life
which have left him depressed in spirit. To this, the Wanderer replies in the
Book called 'Despondency Corrected', from which the following passages are
taken. 'The Excursion' has four further Books not represented in this selection

Here closed the Tenant of that lonely vale
His mournful narrative – commenced in pain,
In pain commenced, and ended without peace:
Yet tempered, not unfrequently, with strains
Of native feeling, grateful to our minds;
And yielding surely some relief to his,
While we sate listening with compassion due.

A pause of silence followed; then, with voice
That did not falter though the heart was moved,
The Wanderer said: —

                'One adequate support
For the calamities of mortal life
Exists — one only; an assured belief
That the procession of our fate, howe'er
Sad or disturbed, is ordered by a Being
Of infinite benevolence and power;
Whose everlasting purposes embrace
All accidents, converting them to good.
—The darts of anguish *fix* not where the seat
Of suffering hath been thoroughly fortified
By acquiescence in the Will supreme
For time and for eternity; by faith,
Faith absolute in God, including hope,
And the defence that lies in boundless love
Of his perfections; with habitual dread
Of aught unworthily conceived, endured
Impatiently, ill-done, or left undone,
To the dishonour of his holy name.
Soul of our Souls, and safeguard of the world!
Sustain, thou only canst, the sick of heart;
Restore their languid spirits, and recall
Their lost affections unto thee and thine!'

  Then, as we issued from that covert nook,
He thus continued, lifting up his eyes
To heaven: — 'How beautiful this dome of sky;
And the vast hills, in fluctuation fixed
At thy command, how awful! Shall the Soul,
Human and rational, report of thee
Even less than these! — Be mute who will, who can,
Yet I will praise thee with impassioned voice:
My lips, that may forget thee in the crowd,
Cannot forget thee here; where thou hast built,

For thy own glory, in the wilderness!
Me didst thou constitute a priest of thine,
I such a temple as we now behold
Reared for thy presence: therefore am I bound
To worship, here, and everywhere – as one
Not doomed to ignorance, though forced to tread,
From childhood up, the ways of poverty;
From unreflecting ignorance preserved,
And from debasement rescued. – By thy grace
The particle divine remained unquenched;
And, 'mid the wild weeds of a rugged soil,
Thy bounty caused to flourish deathless flowers,
From paradise transplanted: wintry age
Impends; the frost will gather round my heart;
If the flowers wither, I am worse than dead!
– Come, labour, when the worn-out frame requires
Perpetual sabbath; come, disease and want;
And sad exclusion through decay of sense;
But leave me unabated trust in thee –
And let thy favour, to the end of life,
Inspire me with ability to seek
Repose and hope among eternal things –
Father of heaven and earth! and I am rich,
And will possess my portion in content!

    'And what are things eternal? – powers depart,'
The grey-haired Wanderer steadfastly replied,
Answering the question which himself had asked,
'Possessions vanish, and opinions change,
And passions hold a fluctuating seat:
But, by the storms of circumstance unshaken,
And subject neither to eclipse nor wane,
Duty exists; – immutably survive,
For our support, the measures and the forms,
Which an abstract intelligence supplies;
Whose kingdom is, where time and space are not.
Of other converse which mind, soul, and heart,

Do, with united urgency, require,
What more that may not perish? – Thou, dread source,
Prime, self-existing cause and end of all
That in the scale of being fill their place;
Above our human region, or below,
Set and sustained; – thou, who didst wrap the cloud
Of infancy around us, that thyself,
Therein, with our simplicity awhile
Might'st hold, on earth, communion undisturbed;
Who from the anarchy of dreaming sleep,
Or from its death-like void, with punctual care,
And touch as gentle as the morning light,
Restor'st us, daily, to the powers of sense
And reason's steadfast rule – thou, thou alone
Art everlasting, and the blessed Spirits,
Which thou includest, as the sea her waves:
For adoration thou endur'st; endure
For consciousness the motions of thy will;
For apprehension those transcendent truths
Of the pure intellect, that stand as laws
(Submission constituting strength and power)
Even to thy Being's infinite majesty!
This universe shall pass away – a work
Glorious! because the shadow of thy might,
A step, or link, for intercourse with thee.
Ah! if the time must come, in which my feet
No more shall stray where meditation leads,
By flowing stream, through wood, or craggy wild,
Loved haunts like these; the unimprisoned Mind
May yet have scope to range among her own,
Her thoughts, her images, her high desires.
If the dear faculty of sight should fail,
Still, it may be allowed me to remember
What visionary powers of eye and soul
In youth were mine; when, stationed on the top
Of some huge hill, expectant, I beheld
The sun rise up, from distant climes returned

Darkness to chase, and sleep; and bring the day
His bounteous gift! or saw him toward the deep
Sink, with a retinue of flaming clouds
Attended; then, my spirit was entranced
With joy exalted to beatitude;
The measure of my soul was filled with bliss,
And holiest love; as earth, sea, air, with light,
With pomp, with glory, with magnificence!

'Those fervent raptures are for ever flown;
And, since their date, my soul hath undergone
Change manifold, for better or for worse:
Yet cease I not to struggle, and aspire
Heavenward; and chide the part of me that flags,
Through sinful choice; or dread necessity
On human nature from above imposed.
'Tis, by comparison, an easy task
Earth to despise; but, to converse with heaven –
This is not easy: – to relinquish all
We have, or hope, of happiness and joy,
And stand in freedom loosened from this world,
I deem not arduous; but must needs confess
That 'tis a thing impossible to frame
Conceptions equal to the soul's desires;
And the most difficult of tasks to *keep*
Heights which the soul is competent to gain.
– Man is of dust: ethereal hopes are his,
Which, when they should sustain themselves aloft,
Want due consistence; like a pillar of smoke,
That with majestic energy from earth
Rises; but, having reached the thinner air,
Melts, and dissolves, and is no longer seen.
From this infirmity of mortal kind
Sorrow proceeds, which else were not; at least,
If grief be something hallowed and ordained,
If, in proportion, it be just and meet,
Yet, through this weakness of the general heart,

Is it enabled to maintain its hold
In that excess which conscience disapproves.
For who could sink and settle to that point
Of selfishness; so senseless who could be
As long and perseveringly to mourn
For any object of his love, removed
From this unstable world, if he could fix
A satisfying view upon that state
Of pure, imperishable, blessedness,
Which reason promises, and holy writ
Ensures to all believers? – Yet mistrust
Is of such incapacity, methinks,
No natural branch; despondency far less;
And, least of all, is absolute despair.
– And, if there be whose tender frames have drooped
Even to the dust; apparently, through weight
Of anguish unrelieved, and lack of power
An agonizing sorrow to transmute;
Deem not that proof is here of hope withheld
When wanted most; a confidence impaired
So pitiably, that, having ceased to see
With bodily eyes, they are borne down by love
Of what is lost, and perish through regret.
Oh! no, the innocent Sufferer often sees
Too clearly; feels too vividly; and longs
To realize the vision, with intense
And over-constant yearning; – there – there lies
The excess, by which the balance is destroyed.
Too, too contracted are these walls of flesh,
This vital warmth too cold, these visual orbs,
Though inconceivably endowed, too dim
For any passion of the soul that leads
To ecstasy; and all the crooked paths
Of time and change disdaining, takes its course
Along the line of limitless desires.
I, speaking now from such disorder free,
Nor rapt, nor craving, but in settled peace,

I cannot doubt that they whom you deplore
Are glorified; or, if they sleep, shall wake
From sleep, and dwell with God in endless love.
Hope, below this, consists not with belief
In mercy, carried infinite degrees
Beyond the tenderness of human hearts:
Hope, below this, consists not with belief
In perfect wisdom, guiding mightiest power,
That finds no limits but her own pure will.

'Here then we rest; not fearing for our creed
The worst that human reasoning can achieve,
To unsettle or perplex it: yet with pain
Acknowledging, and grievous self-reproach,
That, though immovably convinced, we want
Zeal, and the virtue to exist by faith
As soldiers live by courage; as, by strength
Of heart, the sailor fights with roaring seas.
Alas! the endowment of immortal power
Is matched unequally with custom, time,
And domineering faculties of sense
In *all;* in most with superadded foes,
Idle temptations; open vanities,
Ephemeral offspring of the unblushing world;
And, in the private regions of the mind,
Ill-governed passions, rankling of despite,
Immoderate wishes, pining discontent,
Distress and care. What then remains? – To seek
Those helps for his occasions ever near
Who lacks not will to use them; vows, renewed
On the first motion of a holy thought;
Vigils of contemplation; praise, and prayer –
A stream, which, from the fountain of the heart
Issuing, however feebly, nowhere flows
Without access of unexpected strength.
But, above all, the victory is most sure
For him, who, seeking faith by virtue, strives

To yield entire submission to the law
Of conscience – conscience reverenced and obeyed,
As God's most intimate presence in the soul,
And his most perfect image in the world.
– Endeavour thus to live; these rules regard;
These helps solicit; and a steadfast seat
Shall then be yours among the happy few
Who dwell on earth, yet breathe empyreal air,
Sons of the morning. For your nobler part,
Ere disencumbered of her mortal chains,
Doubt shall be quelled and trouble chased away;
With only such degree of sadness left
As may support longings of pure desire;
And strengthen love, rejoicing secretly
In the sublime attractions of the grave.'

Index of First Lines